Voluntary Taxation and Capital Punishment: For a Just, Equal and Corruption-Free Society

Bruce Masters

Copyright information

Thanks for Your Time

Hello, I just wanted to thank you in advance for your time.

I hope there is something positive, entertaining and useful in each of my books for everyone.

If you would like to reproduce any of my books for any reason, in any language or format, please feel free to do so for journalism, education or business purposes—if you can profit from my words, please do so, I will never request royalties.

If you enjoy this book, find it helpful, interesting or educational, please share a copy with a friend or tell others about these books and consider leaving a review or some feedback, which would be much appreciated.

Thanks again for your time. It is very nice to meet you.

Bruce

iv

Introduction

As Tony Benn rather astutely pointed out, politicians and elites/corporations prefer a dumbed-down, addicted, despondent, apathetic and docile citizenry as such a group or herd is easy to manage, take advantage of, boss around, tax and govern.

Being forced to fund the lifestyles and life extensions of the very worst criminals, terrorists and the corrupt is a surefire means to demoralise one and all, whilst change and "progress" frighten many; as Benn said, demoralise and frighten.

In the West we are told that we're headed towards a progressive future, that we are achieving progress all the time. Even as the rates of paedophilia, corruption, rape, terrorism and murder rise exponentially we are told that we are progressing, but progressing to where. A perpetual crime-ridden reality where everyone is raped at least a few times in their lives, where all are victims of corrupt and nepotistic and treasonous politicians, where all are burgled and where soon all are bullied, carjacked and worse, much worse?

This is not progress; this is surrender, apathy and masochistic weakness and being passive.

I say no more to this nonsense; I say "progress" needs to die in order for humanity and peace and order to live and the very first change we need to make is the reintroduction and mass use of capital punishment in every nation.

If you read until the end of this work, you will find it hard to disagree with the proposals and conclusion provided; you will no longer be able to use the same arguments and will find yourself reluctantly agreeing that liberal softness, tolerance and forgiveness and love for rapists in tandem with the philosophy and creed of eternal "progressiveness" is dooming us individually and collectively.

We have all listened to the arguments over many decades in regards to ending or banning capital punishment, so this book is a much needed addition to the debate, especially as it includes information, insight and arguments found nowhere else, which will change everything for the better, which will massively reduce crime whilst massively increasing happiness, trust and harmony in many nations.

Those who refuse to read this book, or any book presenting differing opinions, due to fearing they will become changed as a result have already lost the debate, are in denial and are choosing to remain living in an illusion, living in a fairy-tale existence with their fingers in their ears and their hands placed over their eyes. When you are ready to wake up, ready to listen and read to see the truth, open this book and read from beginning to end. It will make you feel uncomfortable; it may be difficult for you, but you will be stronger and more honest afterwards, no longer in denial, and no longer will your head be in the sand.

Human euthanasia/execution should always be as painless and quick as possible. The primary reason to end the life of a threat to you and your children is to create safety whilst preventing the relatives of the victims and the victims themselves being forced to pay taxes to cover the cost of the eternal imprisonment and care of the criminal anti-society, anti-human offender. Sadism should play no part in executions or justice despite the understandably high level of anger towards the wrongdoer. Justice not revenge, love not hate.

Referendums are a good thing, a loving and empowering thing, and we will get on to the topic of people power and true representative democracy shortly within this work and explore the huge benefits afforded by the introduction of both Capital Punishment and Opt-In (voluntary) Taxation.

***

The purpose of introducing humane capital punishment and Opt-In Taxation (voluntary taxation) is to ensure that law-abiding citizens are not hurt twice, or even three times or more, by crime, corruption, political and judicial failure—once is more than enough.

The sexual assault victim is hurt once by the offender, hurt again by being unable to opt out of funding the prison/probation systems (being forced to pay tax to feed and clothe and house and protect the offender) and then hurt yet again when the offender is released from prison. Hurt, impoverished, slighted, degraded, disempowered, insulted and terrified is how the current experience could be described.

Yet, once the victim is required to opt in in order to pay additional taxes to fund her attacker's prison stay and for him to be rehoused and kept on welfare following his release (which few-to-none would ever volunteer to do), when only those with a deep love for violent and sexual criminals are paying for their life extensions, balance is created, sanity is restored as justice is done.

When a victim of crime, perhaps multiple crimes spanning many years, struggles to pay utility bills, struggles to afford to buy a loaf of bread, whose fault is that?

Is it their own fault as a result of them (instead of becoming a vigilante) reporting crimes to the police, visiting the court to give evidence on multiple occasions and never questioning why they are paying so much in taxes each year, money that benefits criminals in jails who never need to worry about paying for utilities, healthcare or bread?

No. It is not their fault; rather, it is the fault of detached, well-meaning and forgiving and tolerant liberals and members of the clergy and folk who haven't quite thought about how immoral and illogical the system they have created is.

The victim should have the right to choose not to advantage their rapist or the man or woman who killed their father or brother or friend or husband.

The victim should have the right to choose not to buy bread for paedophiles or traitors or terrorists enjoying a paid vacation in prison with no responsibilities, no bills, no rent, no mortgage, no forced labour, no fear of home invasions, no fear of carjackings.

There comes a point when victims say, 'No more.' There comes a point when all of this nonsense tolerance and nonsense masochism, which drags us all down into the gutter, must come to an end. We have now reached that point; *this* is the time for change, immediate change.

The clergy, liberal elites, corporations, billionaires, politicians, political/social activists and the relatives of imprisoned killers and rapists and terrorists and traitors and fifth-columnists can all, if they so choose, opt in to pay higher taxes in order to keep prisons open and to keep the probation service alive. No one will stop such folk from putting their hands in their pockets in search of gold that they wish to lavish upon the very worst in our number. No one will stop them, but all will think them mad.

Gone be the outpourings of compassion for the man or woman found guilty by his peers; gone be the guilt-tripping and outrageous insistence on shared suffering and shared self-abnegation. Those who wish to pay can pay; those who refuse to pay must be permitted to opt out of funding the wants and needs of the very few.

Eventually, those who identify as liberal, woke, progressive, pacifist, socialist, internationalist or humanitarian will get bored of being the only folk who are paying to keep the lights on at the prison, the only ones who are sharing their wages and resources with killers, rapists, terrorists and traitors and paedophiles, and that's when a rather interesting thing occurs— logic and sanity return!

Your experience may be different from my own, me being British and of the working class, born in England. Perhaps you are of another class, whose encounters with violent crime and criminality and bullying and burglaries and psychological terror are limited or even non-existent; if that is so, count yourself blessed.

It has been my experience that the majority of poor folk, those who work manual labour jobs as well as those who subsist off welfare, do not desire for prisons to exist whatsoever but, rather, that profound deterrents and disincentives should exist in order to prevent crime, all crime, in the first place.

Britain was once a peaceful place, it was known that you did not need to lock your front door. The police officer was armed with but his whistle, truncheon and his courage!

But look at her today, look at the USA today; we observe the opposite. We observe the militarisation of the police as new prisons are built each week. They call this "progress".

Are the few who insist on the justice system being infused with liberal tolerance and masochism the only ones paying for this transformation of our cultures and norms? Do they pay for the house alarms, door locks, surveillance cameras and new prisons and ankle monitors all needed as a result of their chosen model of "justice" and "law and order" achieving supremacy? No—you are paying, everyone is paying; this is unsustainable.

This book is an attempt to negate the need for new security infrastructure, to reverse the trend of the surveillance state, to roll back antisocial behaviour and individual protectionism caused by crime waves and an absence of political willpower to smash crime dead. This book is how the silent majority feel. There are few among us who wish to buy terrorists, traitors, paedophiles and killers another meal, which we deliver with a smile to their hotel room in prison. Enough is enough.

If you had witnessed your neighbours' Christmas presents stolen from literally under their tree in your youth; if you have friends or siblings who were dragged off the street and raped by a gang of thugs; if you were robbed at knifepoint or gunpoint in the past; if your home had been burgled by armed men on a dozen occasions you would feel very differently about law and order, very differently indeed.

It is easy to be benevolent when you are detached and removed and comfortable and safe, which is why criminals are never rehomed in privileged elite enclaves or elite gated communities; no, it is always the working class who must suffer, unendingly so.

Respect for the people (and for law and order) must return and love for community and nation must return also as when we live separate, individualistic lives, it is harder to care about the whole, which leads us to unthinkingly release monsters into the community, merely hoping that we, individually, do not become victims of their probable reoffending. Recidivism rates will make harrowing reading for those who put criminals first and the law-abiding folk they terrorise last.

No one does or would advocate a purge (as in the movie of the same name); no one sane would advocate a 'cull' of offenders, that is not the purpose of ensuring the rightful return of capital punishment interlinked with Opt-In Taxation, better known as voluntary taxation, with these things when in place demotivating criminals, setting them on new, peaceful and righteous paths. Insane, self-hating, liberal and masochistic men throw money at criminals and bullies whereas sane and strong men throw shovels and work gloves at them, insisting they contribute like all others or face swift justice.

Which sounds more palatable to you?

A man, driven by guilt or his ideology, chooses to extend the life of an unrepentant serial killer paedophile by fifty years after 'opting in' to pay more tax to fund prisons. He shares the fruits of his labours with the evil-doer, to the detriment of himself and his family and his community, to pay for him to be kept in an air-conditioned cell with a television, free utilities, free food, free medical treatment and free legal aid for life.

Or…

A man, driven by a desire to disincentivise all crime, protect his family, protect his community and avoid becoming impoverished, chooses to end the life of an unrepentant serial killer paedophile by refusing to opt in to fund prisons, just as the vast majority of taxpayers will choose to do, other than liberal elites, the clergy, "progressive" corporations and various privileged categories of folk, especially billionaires. Now with no one being willing to feed or water or house or protect the enemy of humanity, capital punishment returns.

***

Opt-in, in tandem with capital punishment, will assist greatly in ending violent crime, rape and fear, ending terrorism and treason, snuffing out fifth columnism, smashing paedophilia and ensuring no more bars are needed on windows, no new surveillance cameras are needed, no more militarisation of the police is needed, and no more authoritarianism and forced taxation are required to extend the lives of those who have ruined ours. No more.

Yet, such a change as voluntary taxation and capital punishment should not be introduced by a minority on any side; rather, the majority, all of us, should have a vote and say on this crucially important far-reaching issue, which is why Opt-In and capital punishment should be put to the vote. There need to be referendums on these issues. The people, all of the people, must decide their fate and what their culture is and becomes, rather than just the few who are untouched by most criminality and violence, who either do not understand the plight of the common man and common woman or simply don't care.

Honest and wise folk, not in denial, will read until the end of this book, knowing that if they do not, peoples in many nations, if not given the opportunity to protect themselves from crime and egregious taxation (egregious due to it being used to benefit criminals), will either emigrate, choose lifelong welfare subsistence (going on strike nationally, a mass protest to collapse the entire system), or lurch towards the very far left or the very far right.

This. Right here and right now, *this* is an opportunity to save democracies in the West as well as in other places across the world.

This is an opportunity to reassure good folk, an opportunity to restore order and stoicism and sanity and patriotism.

Every criminal should come to be considered to be a traitor. We must adopt a wartime mentality; how can we fight an enemy, an invader, when our own people are invading our homes, raping and robbing and killing us and dealing killer drugs to our children?

We can continue downwards into the gutter as rape becomes punished by a $50 fine and treason punished with a stern telling off, as serial killers are forced to complete ten hours of community service cleaning streets to compensate the people and state for their actions. Yes, we can go on being insanely masochistic; we can nihilistically slit the throat of the state by enacting policies today that will predictably destroy the nation within a century, perhaps within half that time even; yet with newly found strength and courage, born out of desperate need and a desire to save the people and nation, we can avoid calamity. We can avoid the rise of one-party states; we can safeguard the future whilst restoring the natural balance whilst creating true equality merely by offering a referendum to the people on Opt-In Taxation and another on capital punishment.

Do this and all will be well. Do this and democracy will survive. Do this and peace and sanity and community spirit shall return. Do this and the people will take care of the rest.

When Rome was sacked in 1527, it was the Christian tolerance for criminals that ensured every single Roman woman was raped at least a dozen times before being murdered or sold into slavery, why? Because when the invading troops broke through Rome's defences, the first thing they did was release all of Rome's prisoners from her many jails, all of whom enthusiastically joined in with the mass pillage, mass rapes, mass torture and the general debasement of humanity. Tolerance and forgiveness and weakness always doom you in the end.

What is Opt-In Taxation?

Opt-In, or voluntary, taxation is an innovative means to decrease tensions and extremism, prevent extreme partisanism, and stave off insurrections and riots whilst ensuring that the vast majority of folk who pay tax become fully satisfied with life rather than the situation we have at the present time, where only the few, those with savings enough already to sustain them throughout their lives, are satisfied and fulfilled.

Opt-In was birthed due to class inequality and the unequal sharing of burdens, for instance:

Middle-class and elite-class liberals in California may desire to have open borders, may desire to release killers and terrorists and paedophiles from prison after only a few short years, may desire for the nation to accept ten million refugees from faraway lands, may desire US Government forms to be (at great cost to taxpayers) translated into 100 separate languages rather than them just being published in English.

Yet, the working-class conservative who has no savings, who is hurt by recessions and foreign job competitors and who needs to pay as little tax as possible in order to survive and thrive legally, who does not desire government assistance or welfare or 'free stuff', does not desire the same things as his privileged liberal cousins, is confused when his taxes skyrocket as a result of the wants and desires of those from other classes who believe in differing philosophies and competing political positions.

The middle-class liberal in California would hate being forced to pay higher taxes in order to fund a border wall. The working-class conservative in California would hate having to pay higher taxes to fund free housing for millions of illegal immigrants who have entered his nation illegally.

This is where Opt-In Taxation comes in.

It is hard to be truly angry at the government or nation if you are not being bankrupted by sky-high taxes and stealth taxes (violent criminals being released solely into working-class neighbourhoods, for instance, is one such stealth tax or unequal hurt). The student who throws rocks wears a smile when he does so, knowing full well that he should only complain AFTER he has been forced to share the fruits of his labours, too many fruits.

If you are only expected to 'pay for what you want' or 'pay for what you use/need', gone will be true radicalism, gone will be so much hate, with all sides winning as the poor and working class are no longer compelled to fund mass immigration, refugees, abortion, and socialised medicine whilst the privileged and pro-high-taxes liberal elites are now empowered to be able to pay more in tax, far more, in order to get whatever they want. This is true democracy, true equality and fair play.

This type of tax system is known as Opt-In because that is what would be necessary. The taxpayer would suddenly notice their tax bill HALVE overnight, at a minimum, following the implementation of Opt-In Taxation due to many government departments and social programs and liberal wants and foreign aid all falling under the umbrella of Opt-In Taxation and thus all being removed from a person's tax bill.

If the taxpayer thereafter decided they wished to fund 'Obamacare', for instance, they could, easily, by filling out a form or sending an SMS or an email or visiting a government office in order to opt in to fund that department/cause.

If you desire for the government to pay for refugees, foreign aid, abortion, socialised medicine, and free methadone for drug addicts you will be able to tick a box on a simple form in order to pay higher taxes, which will be spent on what you want your taxes to be spent on. Presumably, most folk who desire a bigger state and higher taxes would all opt in to pay higher taxes, whereas those who desire a small state, low taxes and greater individual freedoms and responsibilities would invariably choose not to opt in, not being required to do a thing as they notice their finances improving as the finances of those who choose to opt in to pay higher taxes worsen, creating equality.

Yet, the working-class conservatives, if they desire a new border wall, would be able to opt in to pay higher taxes to fund that project, which middle and elite-class liberals in California would be opposed to, which is why they would not choose to opt in to pay higher taxes to strengthen border security.

The end result of Opt-In will be greater happiness among the working class; everyone getting what they pay for, what they want, and greater equality being achieved due to only the wealthy and privileged paying much higher taxes, which they cannot complain about due to opting in to pay the higher taxes themselves—they can opt out at any time also.

Opt-In applies to individuals as well as businesses and corporations.

Additional Chapters

In this work there are to be found several additional chapters that originally appeared in other books; they are reproduced here due to the included chapters having overlapping themes. Many of my works are interrelated and touch upon the same themes—politics and psychology, sociology and economics, law and order and demographics and democracy and peace.

Including these additional chapters helps to fill in the blanks in certain books whilst giving the reader a small sample of interrelated works in case they desire to read and learn more.

Other reproduced chapters are included to further general knowledge and education whilst creating balance.

Contents

Copyright information...ii

Thanks for Your Time...iii

Introduction iv

What is Opt-In Taxation? x

Additional Chapters xii

Contents..xiii

Chapter One—Why the Future Is Predictable—Including the Result of the Referendum on Capital Punishment 1

Chapter Two—Taxes, Prison Sentences and Deterrents 4

Chapter Three—Questions from a Taxpayer...9

Chapter Four—Immigration 'Opt-In' Taxation System.......................12

Chapter Five—Why the Death Penalty Is So Important and So Misunderstood...19

Chapter Six—What We Should Have Learnt from the Sack of Rome........25

Chapter Seven—Opt-in Taxation for Individuals, Businesses and Corporations 28

Chapter Eight—You Are Too Sensitive 31

Chapter Nine—A Conversation with an Anti-Death Penalty Advocate 35

Chapter Ten—What Would Jesus Do? 37

Chapter Eleven—Jesus and Christians...39

Chapter Twelve—Euthanasia for Lifelong Dangerous Criminals (Who Cannot Be/Refuse to Be Rehabilitated) Is Humane 46

Chapter Thirteen—The 'Push the Button' Scenario 48

Chapter Fourteen—Cognitive Dissonance..50

Chapter Fifteen—Capital Punishment Categories...............................52

Chapter Sixteen—The Confused Anti-Death Penalty Lobby................75

Chapter Seventeen—Protect Me, You F***ing Fascist Scum! 77

Chapter Eighteen—Woke Democratic Hypocrisy 85

Chapter Nineteen—In the News..87

Chapter Twenty—The 'Real Jesus' and Why the Clergy Only Temporarily

Hate Capital Punishment 90
Chapter Twenty-One—More Taxes That Should Go … and Why 96
Chapter Twenty-Two—How to Democratically Silence Fake Saviours and Virtue Signallers Opposed to Capital Punishment 98
Chapter Twenty-Three—Mental Illness and Excuses 101
Chapter Twenty-Four—In the Age of Woke, Is It Ever Appropriate to Tell the Enemies of Humanity to Fall on Their Sword? 103
Chapter Twenty-Five—Pacifists and Anti-Capital Punishment Advocates in a Nutshell 108
Chapter Twenty-Six—What Is Punishment? 111
Chapter Twenty-Seven—The Opt-In Taxation Form..................................115
Chapter Twenty-Eight—Desert Islands Kill Woke Ideology Every Time, Guaranteed..118
Chapter Twenty-Nine—How Woke Creates Hell on Earth........................127
Chapter Thirty—If Jesus Was Without Sin, Why Didn't He Cast the First Stone?..130
Chapter Thirty-One—Leaders Are Never Pacifists or Anti-Capital Punishment 132
Chapter Thirty-Two—How Voluntary Taxation Will Prevent Fascism from Rising Again in the West..135
Chapter Thirty-Three—The People's Protection Contract 140
Chapter Thirty-Four—Death for Treason..148
Chapter Thirty-Five—Restructuring of Welfare, Housing and Healthcare Systems 151
Chapter Thirty-Six—The Death of Silicon Valley and US Corporations..157
Chapter Thirty-Seven—Food for Thought 160
Capital Punishment Conclusion 169
Opt-In Taxation Conclusion...174
About the Author 177
Books by the Author 178

Chapter One—Why the Future Is Predictable—Including the Result of the Referendum on Capital Punishment

'You feel the last bit of breath leaving their body. You're looking into their eyes. A person in that situation is God!'
—Ted Bundy, who killed up to 100 victims and escaped from jail on two occasions in order to continue his killing spree.

If you know enough about history, sociology, criminology, psychology, current affairs, human nature and what key ingredients are required to create and maintain civilisation and good order, it is entirely possible to predict future events, be they months away or years away.

It is my knowingness of a great many things, being a lifelong eager student and now educator and campaigner, that empowers me to be able to see the future.

Evidence of this is found in my predictions of Trump becoming president (which I predicted on the day he ran for office), my prediction that Brexit would become a reality (which I predicted back in 1999), my prediction that COVID would become a pandemic (which I predicted and raised awareness about from as early as January 22nd 2020) and my prediction that Russia would very imminently invade Ukraine (which I predicted on April 3rd 2021) despite all the political and military experts of the time insisting this would never happen—which I evidence within the book *How We Will Create Peace in Ukraine and the World.*

My predictions tend to be accurate. So here is another one:

Capital punishment will soon return to every nation, guaranteed.

My confidence in making this prediction is born out of my knowingness of what occurs in the event of the people, if given the Brexit-style ability to have a vote on capital punishment, choosing to vote NO, rather than YES.

First, let's look at the referendum question.

It will not be so worded; yet, all will know these are the two options:

YES—I want capital punishment to forever exist as a deterrent. I want terrorists and rapists and paedophiles and traitors and serial killers and folk who sell drugs to children to be euthanized legally following a legal trial.

Or…

NO—I prefer to pay higher taxes in order to fund the prison stay, feeding and watering and rehousing, healthcare and welfare of every killer, paedophile, drug dealer, terrorist and violent criminal instead of legally euthanizing threats to my children and to myself and the community. I prefer to share the fruits of my labours with these threats, even when they are unrepentant and bound to reoffend again and again. I even want to aid the life-extension of the very worst and most violent psychopathic criminals who keep committing crimes even after they are released from prison. I prefer to gamble with the safety of my family, community and nation whilst paying higher taxes rather than end the threat and the financial expenditure immediately with a cheap length of rope.

If the people vote 'NO'; if the people vote for higher taxes and greater tolerance for crime, violence and for criminals and recidivism and a supercharged amount of pacifism and neoliberal self-abnegation and self-harm, the floodgates of crime shall immediately swing open as the worst predators in our midst lick their lips and devour the citizenry one by one.

And there can be no complaints from the people, can there, when violent crime soars, when terrorism increases along with rape and murder after the majority voted to be empathic and understanding and forgiving and loving and tolerant towards unrepentant psychopaths and sociopaths who are only ever thinking about creating new victims, about causing new forms of hurt to people, who are only interested in being sadistic and destructive and anarchical and have no desire for community or redemption or rehabilitation.

If people vote against capital punishment, crime rates will rise exponentially; that is the first negative consequence.

The second will be the entire collapse of the democratic system, which will force politicians from all parties, anti-capital punishment advocates/human rights activists as well as many of the worst categories of criminals who were 'saved from euthanasia' to immediately flee to another nation, where they will apply for refugee status out of absolute necessity, and here's why:

It matters not if those against the reintroduction of capital punishment identify as right wing or left wing; if the 'NOs' achieve victory, if capital punishment is defeated, after the very predictable increase in crime and apathy and disorder will come the predictable and inevitable rise of both the far left and the far right.

These forces will either clash or will unite; it would not be hard to bring these factions together, not hard whatsoever.

Once the people vote to be helpless victims, extremists will rise, vigilantes will rise, and the state, rather than attacking and punishing killers, terrorists and paedophiles and traitors and violent criminals and home invaders, will find itself attacking political activists from the left and the right who all desire peace, control and good order.

Martyrs will be created after protests and marches turn violent.

Before long, causes and movements will spring up around the martyrs as communities begin regretting voting in favour of the criminal minority.

These communities will now find themselves joining the marches and demonstrations, which empowers them, raises their spirits and makes them feel like men and women again, rather than like scared mice hiding in their homes from all the violent rapists, gangsters and terrorists just outside their front doors thanks to their liberal, tolerant vote against capital punishment.

Very predictably, clashes will continue until something akin to a putsch is attempted, which will likely fail; yet just as in the case of the Third Reich, it will likely lead to concessions being made and the extreme right-wing or extreme left-wing faction being invited into government, which will be the beginning of the end for democracy of course.

Before long, the only ones remaining in the House of Commons, within the Senate, within every House of Representatives will be those who are willing to die immediately for hard-working, righteous and law-abiding folk.

And what do you think will likely happen next? Yes, capital punishment will be enacted; yet, now, due to it being enacted by fascists or Marxists, new categories of people will be added to the list of those the state wants to euthanize, namely political rivals, pro-democracy advocates, liberal artists, millionaires/billionaires and the intelligentsia....

We can avoid this gloomy, depressing fate by allowing the people a free and fair vote on capital punishment in all democratic nations.

To deny this vote is to court destruction, just as voting the wrong way will guarantee destruction.

Chapter Two—Taxes, Prison Sentences and Deterrents

'The words "I'm sorry" will never come out, for they would be a lie.'
—Joe Metheny, who confessed to killing ten women in the Baltimore area during the 1990s. After befriending and spending time with his victims, Metheny strangled the women to death. He claimed he then used his victims' bodies to create meat patties, which he later sold at a barbecue stand.

(This chapter originally appeared in the book *Ending the Migrant Crisis in Europe: Preventing Class Wars, Race Wars and the Destruction of the EU*)

Currently the deterrents in place are not good enough, not strong enough to prevent potentially millions of illegal immigrants from entering the European Union (and thus nations such as the UK) each year.

The obvious and knee-jerk solution would be tougher sentences for the very serious crimes of people smuggling, drug smuggling and gun running; yet there is a downside to this solution—European taxpayers being forced to pay to keep non-citizens in prison for years or decades. There is no money to pay for this; there is no desire to pay for this.

Instead, it is far better to disincentivise illegal immigration and smuggling of every variety via the use of other means, such as the Opt-in tax system and the reassigning of border security to the armed forces, who will ensure a near 100% reduction in incursions across the EU's southern border.

Whenever one proposes longer sentences, they rarely think about the taxpayers who will be funding these longer sentences. One should always think about taxpayers first, which means implementing many or all of the suggestions offered herein.

Whilst the other recommendations mentioned within this work will indeed reduce instances of people trafficking/sex trafficking in general, there will still be those who insist on trying at all costs to break the EU's rules, why? Because the reward (working in the grey economy in Europe, being able to claim asylum, getting access to free healthcare and welfare in the West) far outweighs the risk of potentially being apprehended.

With this in mind, I suggest shifting the focus away from extended prison sentences (which will financially cripple Europeans) and focusing solely on profiting from the criminals, criminal gangs and smugglers who are undermining the EU in every regard.

If the apprehended individual, who will be considered an invader or trespasser (when a men enters your home without permission, what is he?), possesses assets/property/savings, these things shall be confiscated by the EU immediately, even if doing so requires communication with his homeland to ensure adequate compensation is paid to the EU in order to cover the costs of the translators that were necessary after his/her arrest and the meals and healthcare and lawyers that were all required following their arrest and the accommodation and security personnel who were also needed following their arrest and detention, as well as the cost of the judge or magistrate and a whole host of other combined costs, which in every instance runs into tens of thousands of euros at a minimum.

Those who pay criminal gangs to smuggle them into Europe routinely pay upwards of €6000, this has been widely reported. What this evidences is these individuals, both those who pay to be smuggled as well as those who carry out the smuggling activity, are not poor, not by a long stretch. What homeless German, Brit or Frenchman could muster €1000, let alone six thousand?

Step 1. If illegal immigrants are found in a vehicle and it is established that the driver is complicit in the criminal conspiracy to break a whole raft of EU rules and laws by importing illegal immigrants of absolutely unknown origin, the vehicle shall become the instant property of the EU, it will be sold at auction within seventy-two hours.

Step 2. Any money, valuables, jewellery, mobile phones, laptop computers, electronics in general shall instantly become the property of the EU. The money will be spent on the food and healthcare that the EU generously gives to the criminal group whilst all other seized assets shall be sold at auction within seventy-two hours.

Step 3. All individuals shall be held in detention, without a trial or access to legal counsel, until such a time as the following conditions have been met:

- They each agree to voluntarily leave the EU and never return.

- They each provide detailed information about the criminal networks that operate the people-smuggling, drug-smuggling as well as sex-trafficking operations in the European Union—names, telephone numbers, identities.

- They each give a detailed list of their assets, property and savings and/or a list of the properties and assets and savings of their family members and friends, as well as contact information for all of these individuals—due to the EU incurring extremely high costs every day the uninvited criminal trespassers remain in EU custody.

Step 4. Once the illegal immigrant has compensated the EU fully, they are (at their own expense/the expense of their friends and relatives) instantly deported to their country of origin or the last safe nation they were present within (for instance, Turkey).

Detained illegals would know well in advance that this protocol would be in place. They would know that (if caught) they would be forced to contact their parents in Iraq or their friend in Somalia or their cousin in Egypt in order to have funds wired to the EU in order to pay for the costs of their care and detention and, latterly, to cover the cost of their deportation also.

As a result of this foreknowledge, illegal immigration and smuggling would massively reduce because, suddenly, in order to be free, in order to return to their old lives rather than injecting themselves into another's land without permission, imposing themselves upon EU and UK citizens, they would have to near bankrupt their friends and relatives back at home, who would never think about smuggling themselves through international borders or climbing over border fences. This will act as a huge deterrent due to those back home feeling obligated to help the individual yet angered by having to help them also. Not angered at the EU, no, the EU has done nothing wrong; rather, they will be angered at the criminal who is draining the resources of the EU as the costs of policing, border protection, detention centres, and food and healthcare for non-citizen trespassers skyrocket.

The likelihood of those illegal immigrants who routinely pay thousands of euros to criminal gangs to aid their journey to Europe and the UK not being able to pay for their return journey and to cover the EU's cost of apprehending them, processing them and keeping them in detention for a few weeks are slim to none. These are not poor people; poor people do not have thousands of euros to give to smugglers.

Once the payments have been made, the illegal immigrant should be free to go, yet the cost of release/deportation should exceed what the EU has spent. For instance, if the EU spends €39,000 to apprehend, process, detain, feed and care for a single illegal immigrant for a period of ten days, the cost to the illegal immigrant's next of kin, family members and friends shall be €45,000—the profit would enable the EU to pay for more border fences and more security in general.

The 39,000 euro figure will rise each week, the illegal immigrants would know of this fact before entering Europe illegally, which will cause two things to happen: 1/ They will insist on the most basic form of detention, without perks, in order to keep costs to a minimum because they will be paying for their stay and 2/ It will cause their relatives and friends to reimburse the EU as soon as physically possible, obtaining second mortgages if necessary, selling cars and land if necessary, selling jewellery and televisions if necessary.

In regards to the smugglers themselves, they should (and will) be expected to pay at least double what the individual illegal immigrants are forced to pay, not only compensating the EU fully but also paying such a large fine to discourage any other man or woman anywhere in the world from ever thinking about people smuggling, sex trafficking or drug smuggling or gun running into Europe ever again, totally ending illegal immigration and restoring law and order along all of Europe's borders.

The driver who knowingly smuggles people into Europe will have been paid €20,000. The fifteen or twenty people he illegally brings into Europe have all paid his boss €5000 each—there is a lot of money in organised crime.

The money paid to the low-level smuggler is now forfeit—this belongs to the EU.

The smuggler is held in detention until he identifies his boss. His boss will now be arrested and all of his assets, property, and savings seized and transferred to the EU. Cooperation with third-party nations would be easily facilitated, especially with nations such as Turkey. The Turks are, of course, angered that millions of non-Turks are using their proud nation as little more than a 'staging ground' to enter Europe; how demotivated and depressing this is for Turks, how insulting this is also. Turkey will assist in rooting out criminal gangs, as will all other nations that seek to have friendly relations and good trade with the very influential EU.

Once the first illegal immigrant goes through this process, once they are deported from the EU within less than one week, €30,000 poorer (their family and friends and neighbours as well as themselves €30,000 poorer), illegal immigration will end.

Once the first smuggler goes through this process, €80,000 poorer, the criminal gang they are a part of will splinter and fragment, paranoia and hysteria overcoming them, not knowing what, if anything, the smuggler told the EU authorities about the criminal gang. Within no time at all, such individuals will realise it is far better to start a reputable business or work for an employer than run the risk of losing everything to the EU and their tenacious 'collection department', which soon develops an international reach and everything will be recovered, plus interest.

A typical phone call from a Berlin illegal immigrant detention centre in 2025:

'Hello, Father? Yes, it's me. I have arrived in Berlin, but there is a problem; the EU have captured me. They have taken my valuables and money and my mobile phone, they are looking through all of my contacts on the phone now, soon they will know all about the criminal organisation I used to get to Berlin…. Yes, I know you warned me about this … yes, I am sorry for causing you this stress, but I wanted to come to the EU…. Yes, I know I will have to pay for my stay in Berlin now … yes, I know I will have to pay for my deportation, I knew all of this before I came, I took the risk.

'So, Father, can I please ask you for a favour because I don't want to live in this detention centre? I want to come home; I made a mistake … but be quick with transferring the money because the total increases by the day! Go to my room, there is some money in the green book on the bookcase; take that and sell my computer and furniture and my motorbike from the garage … and I swear I will pay you back for paying for the rest … this is just a loan, I promise. When I come home, I will work harder than ever and I will never leave again … I said I promise … I will never try to enter the EU again, I have learnt my lesson.'

In regards to those who claim they cannot afford to pay for the costs of their stay with the EU and to recompense the EU (and thus working-class and middle-class EU taxpayers) in every regard, they shall remain in detention until pro-immigrant/pro-open border NGOs or those who put the interests of non-EU citizens before the interests of EU citizens valiantly come to their aid by paying to the EU the requisite sum in order to deport the individual in question out of the European Union.

Chapter Three—Questions from a Taxpayer

'One side of me says, "I'd like to talk to her, date her." The other side of me says, "I wonder what her head would look like on a stick."'
—Edmund Kemper, who was convicted of eight murders.

(This chapter originally appeared in the book *Ending the Migrant Crisis in Europe: Preventing Class Wars, Race Wars and the Destruction of the EU*)

An EU voter and taxpayer asks his government a few questions regarding 'Immigration Opt-in'.

'Hello, can we please introduce an Immigration Opt-in tax system in our country?'

'No.'

'Well, in that case, can we have a vote instead on mass immigration and the resettlement of refugees and the sending of our wealth and resources to other nations and to other peoples?'

'No.'

'Could I please ask why?'

'Because Europeans support immigration and helping refugees here and abroad, these are our values.'

'How do you know Europeans support these things? There hasn't been a vote.'

'Only fascists hate refugees and immigrants.'

'The only thing I hate is there not being enough democracy or accountability in my nation. If you were convinced that Europeans support these progressive causes and ideas why wouldn't you allow Europeans to vote in a referendum on this issue and on the issue of continued membership of the European Union, unless you are scared you will hate the results? Do you hate democracy?'

'No one wants to leave the European Union, why would they?'

'Ask Britain that question. If one million people asked you to change the tax system, to make it an Immigration Opt-in system, would you?'

'No.'

'Five million?'

'No.'

'How many people need to request this change?'

'It is not about numbers, we will never allow taxpayers to choose how their contributions are distributed across the world.'

'And the referendum on immigration and on EU membership; if ten million people wanted these referendums (because you refuse to ever so slightly tweak the tax system) would you allow taxpayers to have their vote and their say?'

'No. Our values and principles are unchangeable. If you want more democracy and referendums, the EU will cease to exist.'

'But I thought the EU was a democratic institution designed to help the native peoples.'

'The EU exists to help all peoples; the EU is not racist or selective. You are no different than an African or Asian man, so why should your voice be louder than theirs? Are you racist?'

'I didn't say I am better, I just asked for a referendum because the EU has changed over the years, it in no way resembles the EU of a few decades ago, when it was the ECC (created in 1957 to 'foster economic integration among its member states'). No one, in fact, not a single European ever voted for the European Union, this is the creation of unelected bureaucrats and elites. Can I please opt out of funding mass immigration and demographic change and sending the fruits of my labour abroad?'

'No, but if you are not happy you can leave the EU.'

'Are you sure that blocking the Immigration Opt-in tax system is the right course of action? Every taxpayer is able to tick the box that states, 'I want to opt in to fund every refugee and migrant cause that my elected representatives want me to fund,' so what's the harm? Won't everyone tick the box?'

'But what if no one chose to opt in? Who would help foreigners then?'

'They would have to help themselves, but maybe a few thousand taxpayers would choose to pay more tax, the uber-masochists and self-haters among us, which should be their choice and right. Just as it should be my choice and right not to pay higher taxes to fund migrant and refugee causes, translation and legal costs, accommodation, welfare, healthcare and all the rest of it.'

'No, you are wrong. Most EU taxpayers would warmly welcome the opportunity to pay more taxes in order to help migrants, so if we granted your request for Immigration Opt-In Taxation you wouldn't be happy because only a tiny minority would opt out of funding our progressive and liberal ideological internationalism.'

'So, will you change the tax system?'

'No.'

'But you said most people would choose to pay more.'

'Yes, which is why we don't need Immigration Opt-in because we already know the result because we know how Europeans think and we know what is best for them.'

'Is that the same reason why you don't allow taxpayers to vote on immigration and EU membership?'

'Exactly! Because it would be a waste of time and money, and in any case, Russia would try to interfere in the referendums, or the USA would or China would. There would be election interference, which is why we should have as few votes as possible because democracy can easily be "hijacked".'

'Are you saying that the best thing for me to do is not question anything or complain because there will never be a vote or referendum or change in the tax system and that the many millions who want more democracy should emigrate if having their voice heard and their will enacted is so important to them?'

'Yes, yes, exactly. Anyone who criticises anything the EU does is not welcome in Europe; they are the enemy of progress and liberal democracy. Goodbye.'

Chapter Four—Immigration 'Opt-In' Taxation System

'You constantly think about getting caught, but the rush is worth the risk.'
—David Alan Gore, who confessed to killing six women and wrote letters detailing his murders with grisly quotes. In 2012, they were published in a book.

(This chapter originally appeared in the book Ending the Migrant Crisis in Europe: Preventing Class Wars, Race Wars and the Destruction of the EU)

If you want to pay higher taxes to fund more migrants, more refugees and more external charity endeavours, your country should allow you to pay more tax; the EU should allow you to pay more tax.

If you want to pay lower taxes because you don't want to fund any refugee or migrant cause or external charity endeavour of any kind (for instance, if you are extremely poor and in bad health and not a homeowner) your country should not force you to pay for these things and the EU should not force you to pay higher taxes to fund these things.

Once implemented, the IBTS (immigration-based tax system, also known as the Immigration Opt-in option) would ensure that <u>only those who desperately wished for open borders were expected to cover the costs of housing and caring for migrants and refugees.</u>

No vote or referendum would be required to implement such a dual system as those who wanted to pay for refugees or migrants in general would only be required to tick a box on a tax form in order to signal that they wished to 'put their money where their mouth is' by opting to pay higher taxes in order to help foreigners, whereas everyone else need not do a thing as not ticking the box would ensure an instant tax reduction and thus an opting out of paying to house, feed and protect non-EU citizens.

Opting in would increase your tax from, say, forty to fifty percent; however, this could rise far higher if few others chose to opt in.

Within a fortnight, the results would be in; a referendum would have, in effect, been held on immigration and the result should cause millions of economic migrants to look elsewhere for a new place to live because it is predictable that 99% of people would opt out of paying for non-EU citizens.

Voters/taxpayers could opt out at any time (after opting in), but when this happened, the individual could no longer proudly display the poster in their window, which would read, 'I chose to pay higher taxes.'

If you love immigrants you will pay for them.

If the liberal teachers who regularly strike and protest because they believe they are not paid enough want to pay more tax, they should be allowed to pay more tax if it means helping asylum seekers and unfortunate foreigners. Yet, it is unlikely that such individuals who are at the forefront of the pro-immigration "cause" would be happy if only pro-immigration advocates were expected to feed and house outsiders—because if they were happy to suffer, why would they continually strike and march?

It is easy to shout, 'Let them all in,' when someone else is paying the bill, but when you alone have to pay, the shout soon becomes a muted whisper.

The end result of this common-sense proposal would be as follows:

Where currently the parents of all the children in a classroom pay more or less the same amount of tax (this could be the UK or Germany or France, for instance) as the teacher and headmaster, who are both staunch socialists and pro-multiculturalism and anti-borders, after the small tweak to the tax system everything would change, including the world outlook of the teaching staff.

The parents of the five children whom the teacher classifies as refugees or asylum seekers likely don't work and thus don't pay tax, so no change there.

The parents of several children who were born in other nations who relocated for financial reasons (economic migrants) will now be paying far less tax because they will, understandably, not wish to pay to support refugees or asylum seekers or simply non-working foreign born persons because they are choosing the path of work and sacrifice, so they desire everyone else to do the same.

The parents of the poorest indigenous children will now be paying far less tax because they will not choose to pay tax for the express purpose of importing new job competitors and their children and cousins and uncles.

The only parent in the room who will be paying more tax than before is the teacher, who is married to the headmaster. Both choose to use their principles and conviction and "morality" to decide how much of the fruits of their hard labours should be sacrificed in the interests of benefitting complete strangers who would never choose to pay higher taxes, in any situation, at any time, for any reason.

As the teacher looks around the classroom, she notes that the indigenous children are smiling; there is more money in their household. She notes that the children of economic migrants are smiling also for the same reason; she notes the children of second-generation African and Caribbean immigrants are smiling because no one in that community will ever put foreigners before the needs of their African-European or Caribbean-European children who were born and bred in Europe. And, finally, the teacher notes that the only child in the classroom who is not smiling is her own child, who is one of the pupils.

The teacher asks herself why the other children are happy, celebratory, positive and exuberant when her own child seems dour, demotivated, insecure and unhappy. *Is it because we had to cancel our foreign holidays this year because we chose to do the right thing by opting in to fund refugee centres, translation costs, legal fees, housing, healthcare and education for every foreign-born man, woman and child in the world? Or is it because the children and parents in our street laugh at us relentlessly due to the placard we erected in the front garden that states, 'Proud to pay higher taxes because we love refugees'? Or is it because my child feels disinclined to study hard or work hard because she is facing a future of extremely high individual taxation because she will of course be expected to choose to opt in at the very earliest opportunity because foreigners cannot be expected to save themselves?*

What parents will soon be marching, demonstrating, shouting, threatening strikes and complaining? That's right, only the teachers because after the honeymoon period (of feeling virtuous due to sacrificing a bit of their wealth) is over, once the self-abnegation begins to sting too badly, it is predictable that those who chose to pay higher taxes (who hitherto had always complained that they were not paid enough, perhaps because union fees and foreign holidays are very expensive) would do anything and everything possible to subvert democracy and the will of the majority by once again forcing one and all to pay for refugee centres, for welfare for migrants (who don't know the language or culture and who don't wish to learn these things). Those who initially pay the higher tax rate will soon become fatigued and wearied due to solely bearing the burden that they insisted enter their nation and community.

They will shout and shriek, 'This is not fair. Even though it was only liberal middle-class socialist saviours like me who demanded mass immigration and open borders and the admission of a hundred million or more refugees, the indigenous working class should be forced to share the costs of immigration and globalism, even though these things in no way benefit them. Second-generation immigrants should want to pay higher taxes also; everyone should welcome the opportunity to engage in forced and very selective charity.'

Eventually (it wouldn't take long, we all know this is true), those who initially opted to fund migrants and refugees would soon change their position because paying higher taxes isn't such a great thing when it means you are disadvantaged personally in a myriad of ways whilst your neighbours, who are the same in every way apart from politics and philosophy, enjoy an ever greater standard of living. Hearing champagne bottles continually being opened in neighbouring properties as everyone suddenly found themselves paying 10% less tax would cause the staunchest open borders activist (who finds themselves choosing to pay 10% more in tax) to adjust their priorities and their outlook in order to remain sane and solvent.

If the working class and second-generation immigrants (for instance) joined the very narrow group of middle-class liberals in their mission to 'save the world, one foreign citizen at a time' (a nonsense ambition) those in unions and in teaching and politics and the liberal arts would more happily tolerate their standard of living being massively detrimented due to the sudden tax increase—why? Because such people are communistically minded, they are happy to pay more (to fund their pet projects) so long as everyone else is forced to pay an equivalent rate of tax, with such higher taxpayers insisting that it is democratic to be forced to pay taxes to help non-citizens during a time of mass unemployment and homelessness and home repossessions.

The end result of this proposal (which doubles as a vote on immigration, demographic change, identity and individual freedom) will be fewer than 0.1% of citizens in the long term (the most self-harming, self-hating and masochistic citizens) choosing to pay more tax in order to pay the large refugee/migrant bill.

Those nations who adopt this policy can be assured that migration to their nation and refugee applications will massively drop, quite likely in keeping with the percentage of those who choose to pay the 'immigrant tax' (a tax on personal conviction). If only 1% of a nation's children choose to fund migrants and refugees, one can naturally expect a 99% drop in asylum applications, border incursions, and illegal immigration as well as legal immigration. So the nation with the highest percentage of citizens who opt to pay more to fund non-citizens will become the recipient of the largest number of migrants and refugees, which is guaranteed to cause the upper tax rate to increase monthly, if not weekly, due to migrants now ignoring nations that choose not to pay the higher tax option.

If 10% of Germans consistently chose to opt in to pay 15% higher taxation in order to fund refugees and migrants in every imaginable way, Germany would suddenly become like a flame, like a beacon. She would attract every migrant and refugee on the planet because ten percent of Germany would be declaring, 'We have enough land, properties, food, resources and wealth to share. Come here everyone, we will save you and give you fantastic lives!'

Within three months, the Opt-in tax rate (tax addition) would predictably need to be increased to 20% due to 1/ many Germans choosing to opt out after a few months of deliberate financial self-harm caused by them opting in and 2/ migrants being attracted to the generous Germans without considering, 'What happens when the middle class becomes overly burdened by high taxes caused by mass immigration, multiculturalism and their attempt to adopt the world?'

Within twelve months, millions of migrants will have settled in Germany. The country is at breaking point; its public services are overly strained, classroom sizes have doubled and the additional Opt-in tax rate has now reached 30%, meaning a school teacher in Germany will likely be paying 80% tax a year after opting in, whereas a German taxi driver or labourer will only be paying circa 30% tax.

As those who opt in are forced to pay ever greater amounts of tax in order to fund their dream of a socialist paradise, the newly arrived migrants will make statements such as the one below, intended to show gratitude but also as an attempt to keep the guilt-ridden privileged middle class as their eternal allies:

'We thank Germany for housing us and protecting us. We love all Germans, but we especially love the 10% of Germans who are happy to pay double the amount of tax because they are great and loving and caring human beings and we know this 10% of taxpayers will always be there for us. Thank you.'

Pros and Cons of Opting In—in Brief

Those who choose to pay the additional five or ten percent tax will be automatically thanked loudly and very publicly, including being encouraged to place posters in their windows or placards in their gardens crying out to all of their neighbours the fact that they are the kind of person who is happy to pay more taxes in order to improve the lives of non-citizens.

Those who opt in can of course choose to remain anonymous if for some bizarre reason they don't want people to know that they are heroic, altruistic or masochistic (depending on your point of view).

Despite being able to hide from their neighbours, friends, family and colleagues the fact that a taxpayer has chosen to opt in, which will declare, 'I support mass immigration and I love refugees,' it is assumed that few to none will do so, which will cause a predictable series of events:

All of the individual's neighbours suddenly asking for loans or free money as they share their own hard luck stories, bad memories and collective pain in order to emotionally elicit funds from their "generous" neighbour.

Refugees visiting the individual's property and asking in person for additional help and assistance due to them making it abundantly clear that they will give as much as they can to help foreigners.

Fewer foreign holidays and fewer bottles of champagne for 'champagne socialists'.

***

A typical example of not opting in:

A taxpayer in Germany, Mr Klaus, chose not to opt in; he chose not to place his tick in the box on the paper form; he chose not to text the word 'Yes' to the EU; he chose not to visit his local tax office in order to state 'Yes' in person—because Mr Klaus chose to pay as little tax as possible, knowing that the more tax he volunteered to give to non-citizens the more new non-citizens would be attracted to him and his generosity. Seeking not to become bankrupt and miserable, Mr Klaus simply did nothing, he did not need to vote 'No' because the new tax system was centred around opting in; only those who insisted on sharing the fruits of their labours with foreigners had to text, email, fill in a form or visit their local tax office.

After a period of two weeks, the German government sends Mr Klaus a letter confirming that he hasn't 'opted in'. This achieves two things: It gives him another opportunity to opt in (because he may have forgotten to text/email/fill in the relevant tax form) and it will tell him how much surplus income he will have this year compared to the previous year, if his salary is more or less fixed.

The letter:

Dear Mr Klaus,

Because you have chosen not to opt in, this year you will be paying €4145 less in national taxes.

(He will book himself a holiday immediately or pay to repair his roof.)

If you wish to opt in to help migrant and refugee causes, you can do so at any time via text, postal form or by visiting your local tax office and the German Government will increase your taxes immediately in order to assist those causes, after which you will be sent a revised tax statement.

***

All taxpayers will be told how much they will save if they don't 'opt in'.

Automatically, every taxpayer is opted out; they will have to return a form (or text or email/phone or visit their tax office) in order to guarantee their participation in the voluntary 'pro-immigration and pro-refugee tax'.

EU politicians and bureaucrats (and the leaders of non-EU countries who wisely choose to adopt the proposal also) will be blameless in regards to the democratic change because they merely gave taxpayers a choice.

Why having a vote on the adoption of 'Opt-in' is undemocratic.

EU nations shouldn't hold a vote on implementing Opt-In Taxation for one very important and obvious reason: Because millions of EU citizens do not pay tax in any form and millions more benefit from mass immigration—the asylum lawyer will of course vote yes to more immigration, as will the slum landlord, as will recent arrivals who have been granted citizenship, as will those who hate Europe and seek for it to be changed or destroyed.

This change only concerns taxpayers; this only concerns contributors, which is why a vote is unnecessary and undemocratic. In this rare instance, however, of course the majority of taxpayers will certainly vote in favour of the Opt-in system.

Any change to the tax system only concerns taxpayers. Simply requiring taxpayers to opt in is enough to ensure democracy and equality throughout the EU. Those Europeans who are depressed by, displaced by and disadvantaged by mass immigration, demographic change and native flight deserve to be able to choose whether or not they should continue to be forced to fund the things that cause them to be miserable, apathetic and despondent.

Chapter Five—Why the Death Penalty Is So Important and So Misunderstood

'I'd rather be fishing.'
—Jimmy Glass, who escaped from jail and shot an elderly couple to death while burglarizing their home. These were his last words before being executed by electric chair.

(This chapter originally appeared in the book *Defeating Fentanyl*)

Am I aware that currently, in certain places, the death penalty is considered extremely taboo and 'off the cards' and not something any government would allow the people to vote on via a national referendum?

Yes, I know it is taboo in many places, yet I must be honest in regards to capital punishment/the death penalty as despite this subject causing many to dwell on their own mortality and on the feelings of the terrorist or murderer or rapist or paedophile, which causes them to insist it is better to continue releasing everyone from prison, which creates eternal recidivism from now until the end of humanity, which will happen far sooner when you fail to cut cancer out of the tribe when given the opportunity, it is something we must at least consider as a means to prevent repeat offences of terrorism, rape, paedophilia, murder and political corruption.

When one thinks about a huge industrialised nation, be it the UK or France or most states in the USA, they believe things like rape and murder and paedophilia 'normalised' and 'tolerable' (the more liberal and privileged they are the more they think his way) as a result of being somewhat removed from the case, physically and emotionally.

Yet, the man who today says, 'Steady on, Bruce, it took us a long time to finally ban the death penalty. So what if that is a green light for rapists and paedophiles and killers,' should bear in mind that most of those he doesn't wish to kill would remain peaceful and harmless if they knew they would be killed after committing the crime in question. The man needs to be told that the rapist wants to rape one million people, if possible; liberalism and the nanny state and 'rights for all' (even for those who don't follow the rules) enable this.

When a nation educates her citizens to know, from the very beginning, that if they break certain rules and laws, all of their rights, including their right to life, will be revoked immediately as well as their citizenship, no one can defend the killer or rapist as they are no longer a citizen and no longer have rights; now they are merely a human predator, a danger to any society.

If there are 1,000 self-hating people outside the prison, protesting against the execution, go out to them with the man who raped and killed fourteen women and two children and say to them, 'Which one of you will house this man and become responsible for him and feed and clothe him and ensure he never reoffends? And if he does reoffend, are you willing to be jailed for the remainder of your natural life as a result and forfeit all of your property and possessions and wealth, where you will be sharing a prison cell with the detritus you tried to save but who (entirely predictably) turned on you and began raping and killing again?'

Within sixty seconds, the 1,000 people will very quietly slink away and will never be heard from again—because up until that point they were psychologically projecting, believing that every paedophile and killer could be rehabilitated (or they wanted to believe it as it gives more credence to their belief system and lessens cognitive dissonance as a result). They know they can exert self-control so imagine others can also; they know they choose the path of light so imagine others can also. Yet some are born with no light within them, no ability to experience emotions or empathy, and these individuals, after committing serious crimes, will always reoffend, always.

When someone else is paying for the rapist or murderer or paedophile or treasonous politician or spy to be housed, those who are anti-death penalty want him to be kept alive in perpetuity, often outliving their victims, which I consider adding insult to injury.

When someone else is responsible and accountable for the rapist or murderer or paedophile or treasonous politician or spy, those who are anti-death penalty want him to be kept alive in perpetuity, often outliving their victims, which I consider adding insult to injury.

For instance:

If a rapist escapes prison and rapes again, liberals will certainly blame the prison and demand the governor be fired, maybe even charged with criminal negligence; yet when a rapist is released from prison due to liberalism and weakness and short-sightedness and due to a fundamental misunderstanding about good and evil and rapes again, liberals have no one to blame but themselves, yet they do not blame themselves. In fact, they blame no one because each time the rapist rapes, they give him a brief 'time out' in a luxury prison where he is not forced to work twelve hours per day, hard labour, as should be the norm everywhere on planet Earth.

A man is thinking about raping a liberal in a liberal country. The liberal says they don't want to be raped, that they are a pacifist. The non-liberal rapist gives the liberal pacifist a gun, telling her or him (rape affects all, hurts all, destroys all):

'I am giving you the ability to stop me; if you don't kill me, I will rape you.'

It is obvious what happens next; liberalism and pacifism give their consent to being hurt because they care more about rapists than themselves or society.

The rapist walks away after committing yet another crime against humanity and says, 'You still have the gun, I would advise you shoot me in the back, otherwise I will go on raping you know, because I don't have empathy, I don't care how many lives I destroy, I positively revel in it in fact.'

What happens next?

Liberalism and pacifism do nothing because they hate guns and responsibility.

As a direct result, other folk, including liberals and non-liberals, get raped and destroyed because of their refusal to be responsible, due to them not wanting the scumbag's death on their conscience, due to wrongly believing that all humans are equal and equally deserving of life.

This is unnatural, disorder and wrong. It is a cult of suicide; it is self-hating and self-destructive in all ways.

If the criminal has feelings, this is a different matter. Yet, when there is no emotion, no remorse and an absolute inability to empathise and he/she commits crime whilst sober and in control of his/her faculties, the individual will remain a danger to all for the remainder of their lives.

Prison seems like the logical choice, yet who is paying for this?

If it was only liberals who were paying for the prison system (as I believe it should be, especially in the case of rape, paedophilia, murder, terrorism and spies), then I would have no complaint. Yet, when all are forced to pay to keep alive people who they want to be executed because intelligent, hard-working illiberal people don't wish to become impoverished, don't wish to share the fruits of their labours with bad guys, the system becomes unequal, bloated, corrupt and despised by all.

If liberals alone were expected to fund the life-extensions of the worst offenders such as killers and rapists, real predators, a funny thing would occur—they would suddenly be more open to listening to the valid arguments in favour of the implementation of the death penalty.

They would be poor if forced to fund rapist lifestyles and paedophile lifestyles and the lifestyles of murderers, they would not like being poor.

The liberal pacifist is only a liberal pacifist because they have the luxury of being a liberal pacifist. For instance, every one of the survivors of Uruguayan Air Force flight 571, which crashed into the Andes Mountains in 1972, may have been liberal pacifists and non-meat eaters and certainly not cannibals, yet as they each approached death, natural instinct kicked in, and they chose life, rather than death, by becoming cannibals temporarily.

Who Wants the Death Penalty Banned?

Let us imagine it exists everywhere, just as it one day did, because our ancestors were smart people and self-sacrificing and knew that certain folk only understand one thing.

If you were a priest who feared being caught for paedophilia, you would want the death penalty removed.

If you were a CEO of a company you knew damaged the health of many, which could even kill one day also, you would want the death penalty removed.

If you were a rapist or serial killer, you would want the death penalty removed.

If you had never thought about the death penalty for any great length of time or why it was first introduced due to an unknowingness about the dangers of psychopaths and sociopaths and those who are sadists and nihilists, you would want the death penalty removed.

If you had a guilty conscience, had committed crime before or could not trust yourself not to commit crimes in the future of any kind or type, even minor crimes, you would want the death penalty removed.

I dislike killing mosquitos, as they are alive, yet it is unnatural for me to allow myself to be bitten, so when I kill, it is justified. I would hate to kill a lion, but I must put myself and humans first so would kill the lion using any means in order to extend the life of humanity.

Following conviction, those who have committed suicide by breaking society's and humanity's rules should not fester (at great expense to the taxpayer) for thirty years on death row, the execution should occur immediately. 'Bad apples' positively enjoy prison, look how happy Charles Manson is, and review the research of the psychologists and psychiatrists who examined Ted Bundy, who was unapologetic. In fact, it has been reported that Bundy seemed pleased with what he had done as his eyes tuned black when discussing his inhumanity—which has since been attributed to extreme pupil dilation, suggestive of the predator deriving pleasure from recalling his atrocities. Such individuals must be executed immediately, their continuing existence serves no useful purpose to themselves or others, they drain resources whilst certain to reoffend if ever released. Life imprisonment is not a 'nice' third position; it is life in prison, unenviable by the vast majority. Bundy (or at least a part of him) was suicidal, deliberately relocating to Florida only because he knew Florida had the death penalty:

'When I was in Aspen, after his first escape … he asked me where a person would go to actually get the death penalty. I thought that was an odd question to say the least, and I responded, "Oh, Florida or Texas."'—John Henry Browne, Ted Bundy's attorney.

Soon after this exchange, Bundy escaped and moved to Chicago, Ann Arbor then to Michigan before arriving in his final destination, Florida, because, in his attorney's words, 'He knew he was a bad person who needed to be stopped,' and in Bundy's own words, 'I want to be a good person, I'm just not.'

Immediate execution, a bullet, would suffice. There will always be volunteers to enact the will and judgement of the majority, yet a simpler solution is to only keep one killer in prison, who becomes the executer of all other killers, apt and ironic. A single imprisoned rapist could be responsible, for instance, for killing all rapists.

We need to be strong if we want our civilisations and cultures to survive. Good men do not desire to end human life, yet they know that sometimes this is necessary for the common good and a necessary sacrifice in order to keep innocents safe and optimistic and free and joyful. Only cowards, those spoilt and ruined by privilege and entitlement and anti-patriots would refuse to be a hangman, as by their actions the tribe will either be further terrorised by the reoffending career criminal or impoverished by being forced to pay higher taxes in order to feed and house and clothe and provide medical care to the criminal who will likely outlive all of his victims as a result—as they must work hard outside the prison walls in order to pay tax to fund the life extension of the man or woman who wronged them and caused them great trauma and long-term psychological damage.

Those who would march against the reintroduction of the death penalty should be the only people in the community who should pay for killers and paedophiles and terrorists and rapists and spies and corrupt politicians and drug dealers and pimps and people smugglers and drug smugglers to be housed, fed, nurtured and educated—everyone else will happily pay less tax immediately. In this scenario, reoffending rates will remain the same; yet if liberals and the other categories of folk who hate the death penalty are not happy about footing the bill alone (which would bankrupt them and make them miserable and finally anti-criminal and pro-victim) the rates of reoffending would drop massively as all prisons were closed overnight and the worst killers and rapists rehoused exclusively in middle-class and upper-class areas.

Predictably, liberals and similar defenders of criminals would become victims of those they cared so much about again and again until eventually they would be forced to grow up and become responsible and strong and snap out of their daydreaming when they no longer had the luxury of choosing to be benevolent as that benevolence was in fact undemocratic shared benevolence and mercy and tolerance, as when the liberal alone must foot the bill for the eternal housing of rapists and paedophiles and murderers in his own street, in the house next door to where his family live, his liberalism will slip away, it will be cast off into the gutter where it belongs as he tells the anti-human element threatening to destroy his entire world, 'No!'

If a small percentage of folk continue to dictate policy in regards to the death penalty (because the majority are pro-death penalty) governmental policy in regards to the rehousing of killers and paedophiles and rapists and terrorists should change immediately everywhere, taking into account the areas and classes of folk who cannot afford to fund the housing of these groups of undesirables and who desire the death penalty as a deterrent and as the final ultimate form of justice in the land, which restores confidence and hope and brings peace to victims and their families whilst serving to increase the bank balance of victims of rape and paedophilia, for instance, throughout the course of their lives—because they were not required to pay higher taxes to pay for their abuser to be housed and fed and entertained and educated and protected and catered for in every discernable way, in the most humane and sensitive and caring way possible, of course.

Governments should only rehouse those who would have been executed for the crimes only a few short decades ago (before the rise of neoliberalism) in liberal communities, in privileged and wealthy and peaceful communities, rather than in working-class underprivileged communities, which hitherto has been the norm.

Once liberally minded folk observe twenty-storey apartment blocks being erected next to their homes in their protected and exclusive enclaves, which will be filled with 500 killers and paedophiles and rapists and terrorists, they will immediately put out of their mind any foolish notion of 're-education' or 'rehabilitation' or 'early release with an ankle monitor'. Immediately they will either demand to pay higher taxes themselves in order to keep their new neighbours in a prison facility one million miles away or, more likely, will join the ranks of the sane who love their children and community and tribe by calling for the reintroduction of the death penalty. On that day neoliberalism will die as good folk and innocent folk become protected as hope and optimism soars as confidence and pride and justice do also.

Chapter Six—What We Should Have Learnt from the Sack of Rome

'Well, gentlemen, you are about to see a baked Appel.'
—George Appel, who was convicted of first degree murder for killing a police officer. While getting strapped to the electric chair, he suddenly found the situation humorous and delivered those infamous last words.

If you don't know history, you will struggle to understand people and thus will never feel safe and thus will become more warlike.

If you don't know psychology, you will struggle to understand people and thus will never feel safe and thus will become more warlike.

Yet, if you neither know history nor understand psychology, you will never be able to understand people and thus will be fated to war forever until defeated or until everyone else is dead.

The following information is of crucial importance to those who wish to prevent history from always repeating itself. Knowledge is power.

***

Rome has fallen several times throughout the centuries, yet she was sacked dramatically twice in her history, most recently by the Spanish and Holy Roman Empire in 1527, resulting in horses being stabled in St Peter's, forcing the Pope to flee and later pay a huge ransom to be released from imprisonment. It led to unimaginable chaos and disorder as convents were transformed into brothels and cardinals were suspended by ropes over the Tiber River, threatened unendingly with drowning unless they paid huge ransoms.

A far earlier sacking, however, was arguably even more barbaric and gruesome. It occurred in the year 476, when German tribes reached the gates of Rome. The barbarians at the gates used cruel and unusual methods to demotivate, demoralise and to terrify the protectors of that city to allow them inside.

Eventually, as a result of the barbarism and inhumanity, the defence of the city fell and what followed was violent anarchy and disorder, anti-civilisation and score-settling, which ended in huge loss of life and deep collective psychological/spiritual suffering and trauma.

When Rome fell in 1527, the invader similarly employed cruel tactics against the inhabitants of Rome, be they soldiers or priests, bakers or housewives—none were spared. It was a massacre, with the bloodlust and hatred and envy and anger driving the invaders ever forward, guaranteeing that everyone on the other sides of the protective walls would be put to the sword, or worse, once the stalemate was finally broken after the Swiss Guard's valiant defence was shattered by superior numbers and brutal tactics:

"Men were tortured to reveal the hiding places of their possessions or to pay ransoms for the sparing of their lives, one merchant being tied to a tree and having a fingernail wrenched out each day because he could not pay the money demanded.

"Many were suspended for hours by the arms [wrote Francesco Guicciardini's brother, Luigi]; many were cruelly bound by the genitals; many were suspended by the feet high above the road or over the river, while their tormentors threatened to cut the cord. Some were half buried in the cellars; others were nailed up in casks or villainously beaten and wounded; not a few were branded all over their persons with red-hot irons. Some were tortured by extreme thirst, others by insupportable noise (noise torture) and many were cruelly tortured by having their teeth brutally drawn. Others again were forced to eat their own ears, or nose, or their roasted testicles and yet more were subjected to strange, unheard-of martyrdoms that move me too much even to think of, much less describe. …"

—From the book *Rome: The Biography of a City* by Christopher Hibbert

These people who engaged in these wildly inhuman and violent acts, these 'types of people' still exist of course—there are some who love blood and pain and torture and witnessing dog fights who live in your city. Do not deceive yourself, do not think yourself living in a new enlightened period devoid of psychopathy and sadism and pure human evil as it is all around us. This is no Disney production; this is the real world—wake up!

It is extremely foolish and in fact individually and collectively suicidal to ever imagine the evil-doers of the past as being birthed by dragons or goblins or monsters or merely coming to be solely as a result and by-product of ill intent and malice. No, these barbarians who debased humanity were born of women, had fathers, had priests and had dreams and wants and felt pain, felt cold and may have been beggars once. Many gentle folk back then and many today would show pity towards, help and aid them and thereafter be stung by the real them.

These people still walk among us. They are in your prisons; they are in your governments; they are in your law offices; they are in your communities; they are in your schools and temples. Monsters are everywhere, which is why we must guard ourselves now and always and this requires strength as well as honesty. With blinkers on, with rose-tinted glasses on our noble and benevolent and superior and virtuous liberal faces, we will be fated to repeat the mistakes of yesteryear. With blinkers on, Rome will be sacked again and again and again and again and again.

Chapter Seven—Opt-in Taxation for Individuals, Businesses and Corporations

'We've all got the power in our hands to kill, but most people are afraid to use it. The ones who aren't afraid control life itself.'
—Richard Ramirez, a rapist, killer and burglar, known as the 'Night Stalker', who frequently targeted the homes of elderly women.

(This chapter originally appeared in the book *Defeating Fentanyl*)

Imagine, just for a moment, that taxation was only 5% across the board in San Francisco for employees at all levels and business owners and corporations. Would there exist a massive fentanyl epidemic on the streets of San Francisco? The answer is no.

High taxes and liberalism = mass homelessness, mass drug and alcohol abuse, mass entitlement and belligerency and mass disorder and societal collapse.

What if taxation in San Francisco was 95% for everyone, would that fix the problem? No, it would have the direct result of ending liberalism forevermore in San Francisco as previously pacifistic and liberal men and women would take to the streets armed with whatever they could carry as a means to drive out the forces (which are often external) that had caused their taxes to massively increase, becoming wild, becoming feral as they realised the results of all their hard work and self-sacrifice were poverty caused by a minority of folk who only take and never contribute.

The solution to the woes facing places such as San Francisco might just be Opt-in taxation.

Imagine you are a small business owner who faces the prospect of closing your family-run business in San Francisco, which has existed for five generations, as a result of rampant thefts committed by 'untouchable' and 'above the law' and 'protected' hard drug users who are systematically undoing civilisation.

Would you, if given the choice, choose to pay for safe spaces for those who are destroying your business and society? Would you, if given the choice, choose to pay for NGOs to provide homeless drug addict criminals who steal from your family business every day with warm clothes and new tents, which enable their continuing hedonism, self-harm and life of crime and disorder?

The answer is obvious. The answer is, if given the choice, all sane and contributing members of society would choose to opt out of contributing to any schemes that benefitted the bane of their existence, the anti-social, anti-society, self-centred and feral fentanyl and heroin euphoria-chaser and responsibility shirker.

If in San Francisco it became necessary to tick a box on a form or make a phone call to 'opt-into' paying higher taxes, which would be spent on helping the people who are destroying your business and communities and well-being and quality of life and happiness, only a very few would make that call, only very few would tick that box.

The end result of this change would be the small business owners' taxes halving, which would keep them afloat and offset the harm caused by the liberal-backed drug users who habitually steal from small businesses whilst deterring customers from visiting the business due to their presence just outside as they are camped on the sidewalk, loud, gregarious, aggressive and demanding 'free stuff' eternally.

The billions currently awarded to fentanyl users and NGOs as a result of far-too-high taxation suddenly remaining in the pockets of San Franciscans would cause demotivation to NGOs and fentanyl users alike. It would send a clear message that San Francisco wants to survive and thrive, rather than co-exist with feral anti-society elements and the enablers of those anti society elements—liberals, NGOs, compassionate narcissists and sociopathic opportunist profiteers looking to make a quick buck.

This is democracy. This is the logical path for places such as San Francisco that are currently on a downward spiral of surrender and apathy and lowliness. Once every citizen has to opt-in to funding those programs that liberals insist tax money is spent on, those programs and initiatives (which are pointless, which only multiply suffering and waste everyone's finite time and resources) will be defunded overnight.

Then we will know the real San Francisco. Then we will know the real spirit of those people, beyond the nice facades and claimed nobility and unlimited compassion and unbridled tolerance for the intolerable and criminal.

Businesses small and large would choose not to pay to fund NGOs via their taxes, having the result of substantially lowering their taxes immediately.

A predictable snowball effect would occur as taxes massively decreased far and wide, with businesses able to spend the additional funds on massive security measures, for instance, to deter crimes being committed against them, contributing to chronic drug use/addiction being starved as those who refused to sober up would receive no handouts, no help and would no longer be able to steal and would no longer be given 'charity at gunpoint' by passing San Franciscans as begging would predictably end the day Opt-in-taxation went live, owing to a change in community psychology and outlook naturally taking place. All hard-working folk would suddenly feel empowered and strong and in control of their lives and destiny after choosing not to fund the lives and wants of drug addicts.

If the man is not able to steal, if the man is not given handouts, he has three choices if he insists on continuing to be a fentanyl or heroin user: become sober, leave town in search of a more liberal/tolerant/short-sighted town, or commit crime.

If he chooses to become sober, great, we should love and embrace and congratulate him!

If he moves to another town, send him a copy of this book....

Crime (drug-related crime of any kind) = immediate prison.

Good people of San Francisco and of all liberal enclaves being ravished by drugs and addiction, stop surrendering; stop this weakness and dereliction of duty. Get off your knees and demand your community is saved. Think of the next generation, think of your children whom you should love and cherish, they are inheriting the problems that occurred on your watch. No more of this.

Fight back, save yourselves and those lost to addiction. We can save everyone, but only if we are grown-up, strong, resolute and unflinching in our resolve to end this blight once and for all.

Chapter Eight—You Are Too Sensitive

'I believe the only way to reform people is to kill 'em.'
—Carl Panzram, who confessed to killing three young boys and later said he killed twenty-one people. After beating a man to death at Leavenworth Federal Penitentiary, he was sent to death row.

Elites are not influenced by the working class or those who live on the streets or those who live hand to mouth; rather, it is the other way around, which is why everyone in our modern interconnected Western-corporate-Hollywood-feminist-dominated culture has become harmfully overly sensitive and harmfully 'soft' (nice), affected, pampered and thus dangerously weak and vulnerable to being dominated by the dark forces in our midst: psychopaths, sociopaths, narcissists, gaslighters and cunning criminals with sob stories.

Traditionally, the king, the nobles and elites were bloodthirsty because to reach the top you have to fight, you have to kill; just as our species had to fight tooth and nail to become the alpha species.

These days, however, a trend has developed whereby leaders and elites in general have become accustomed to someone else killing their food, preparing their food, cooking their food and then presenting their food.

The privileged and decadent few at the top always desire new ways to prove their supremacy to others and one way is not to have to pluck feathers from birds, not to have get blood on themselves when they are killing or preparing food, not having to gut or descale fish and not having to ever witness in their entire lives an animal or creature of any type or variety being killed.

Elites desire pleasure, meaning there are still elites who kill, as in for trophies, and most such folk will be on psychopathic or sociopathic spectrums or are merely overcompensating for something, or a few somethings.

Yet, on the whole, in recent decades the trend has been for those who have serious money, influence and standing to seek out pleasure by outsourcing any and every job, however small, including killing, preparing and cooking food.

At this point, some may say that animals are not food, to which I say lions consider you food, just as sharks consider you food, and if you leave your new-born baby lying out alone in the grass, a passing eagle will certainly consider your baby food and immediately snatch it and that will be the last you see of your precious treasure.

Animals are food just as grass is food and the pleasant aroma produced when you mow the lawn is a result of chemical defences being released because the grass is in distress.

We kill when we walk on grass, with each footfall certainly killing one hundred small insects and creatures—just as we commit literal genocides when we shower or pluck our eyebrows as tiny creatures (who live in our eyebrows) are accidentally killed when we enjoy a pleasant warm shower or when we unthinkingly pluck a hair and discard it upon the ground.

Caring about every life form drives you insane, you must put the needs and wants of grass and the tiny insects living in your eyebrows last, absolutely last, if you wish to be happy in this world. You cannot cry after accidentally stepping on an ant or a worm; you must care about you.

You must choose stoic survival and an even-tempered existence in which you love and protect your family and friends if you desire true happiness, relaxation or anything close to self-actualisation.

We kill when we plant vegetables in the ground, accidentally killing worms and moles and so many other subterranean creatures.

Death is a part of life, it is unavoidable, yet to focus on the suffering of worms or cows or pigs will drive you insane for no good reason. You must focus on the longevity and health of yourself, your family, friends and community first and foremost, always, wherever you are, whoever you are, <u>even if you are my enemy</u>.

Vegans may state that they survive just fine without killing, yet a distinction must be made as all vegans, especially in the West, where most reside, are of course complicit in killing, despite most not realising it.

Vegans and vegetarians don't want to kill and do not want their food to come to them as a result of death or creatures being killed; yet, when a meat-eating delivery driver drops off vegan ready meals at a vegan or vegetarian's house, meals that are made by meat eaters fuelled by cheese and dairy and meat products, of course there was meat and dairy and animals being used for food as part of their food chain.

Those who claim to be ruled by ethics and morals in this regard are being dishonest with themselves as they are protected by meat eaters in terms of the police and the armed forces, yet they insist on declaring themselves non-violent, pacifists even, and opposed to any killing of any animal (or violent, dangerous criminal) whatsoever for any reason—but of course they would kill a wolf trying to attack and kill their family, surely?

Surely they would kill a black widow spider if it approached their baby's crib?

Those whose diets are born out of ethical concerns or unregulated emotions or bleeding-hearted liberalness, excessive privilege, self-abnegation and monotropism need to conduct an honest self-assessment as, currently, most of these folk, of whom I have met a great many, are psychologically torturing themselves because it is impossible to create a non-violent society, let alone a non-violent world as this world is built on violence.

Civilisation only exists due to our titanically strong and brave ancestors who defeated wolves and sabre tooth tigers and woolly mammoths and snakes and all manner of other dangers to our collective survival.

I have been a vegetarian and vegan previously, finding both diets contributing to depression and self-abnegation and not being conducive with the survival of the human species but very helpful in terms of virtue signalling, guilt/responsibility avoidance, perpetuation of elitism and increasing individualistic grandiosity.

***

When we see elites sitting in restaurants, it is predictable that the middle and working class will similarly desire to eat in restaurants also (envy/jealousy/keeping up with the Joneses/masking/mimicking) rather than hunt or fish for food as was the case for the preceding 100,000 years of human glory, human strength, human self-sacrifice and human indomitability, responsibility and independence.

And then elites had the "clever idea" of globalisation and introducing huge supermarkets because these things were good for maximising products, yet a direct negative consequence of this sudden change was the pampering/nannying of the consumer, with folk in the West now regularly disgusted when they see bones in their food, with the trend now being for everything to be unnaturally boneless.

The folk who "need" their food to be boneless are the same ones who are sickened by the thought of rapists and murderers and corrupt politicians being hung as they prefer to remain delusional and in deep denial, living in a fantasy dream world where wolves don't bite, where ticks and black widows don't bite, where paedophiles never reoffend and where everything should be bloodless and boneless because we are all so sensitive and squeamish and privileged and entitled to be happy at all times. We insist on having the bones and blood and guts and feathers and reality taken away by other people far away who are paid good money to change reality to make consumers smile like mad fools and to take away any feelings of guilt or responsibility for being directly involved in the death of an animal—supply and demand.

When elites are strong, honest, and reject privilege and pampering; when they fish, hunt and have a 'die on your feet' attitude, all men feel and behave this way also. Yet, when elites are woke neoliberals who are always smiling, with manicured fingernails, who have 100 servants, of course the man at the very bottom will envy and replicate that which should never be replicated—and what is created is a nation of co-dependent weaklings only ever consuming processed, boneless meat like babies, in need of nannying, who are disgusted by blood rather than blood being a normal part of life, just like bones; just like legally executing traitors and terrorists and murderers and paedophiles and corrupt politicians should be a normal part of life.

Chapter Nine—A Conversation with an Anti-Death Penalty Advocate

'Warden, murder me. I'm ready to roll. Time to get this party started.'
—James Lewis Jackson, who strangled to death his wife and his two stepdaughters.

Hello, I hear that you are opposed to the death penalty, is that correct?

Yes, very opposed. I hate capital punishment; I want every man and woman to live, even if they rape and kill people or sell heroin and fentanyl to children or are traitors or fifth-columnists or corrupt.

So you will stand outside the prison where rapists, paedophiles, terrorists, treasonous public servants and murderers are awaiting execution and attempt to prevent the deaths of the rapists, paedophiles, terrorists, treasonous public servants and murderers?

Yes, I will stand against any kind of capital punishment, there is never a justification.

In that case, are you willing to house a rapist, a paedophile, a terrorist and a hard drug pusher, for them to live with you and your family today?

Well, no, I do not want that.

But you don't want these threats to you and your children to be killed either?

Correct. I do not want to be responsible for them and I do not want anyone to hurt or kill them.

So, what do you want to happen, or do you believe that nothing should happen after you rape or kill or commit treason or corruption in public office?

They should be punished by going to prison then rehabilitated, educated, loved and released as soon as they are proven to no longer to be a threat to people.

At that time, then, when you say they are rehabilitated and ready to return to the community, will you consent to rehabilitated rapists, paedophiles and murderers and traitors and enemies of the state and terrorists living with you and your family, or living in the house directly next to your house, or in the very next apartment, your brand-new neighbours?

No! I want them to live far away from me.

Okay. I think I understand. Will you consent to the rehabilitated rapists, paedophiles, murderers and terrorists becoming school teachers at your children's school or school caretakers following their rehabilitation?

No, I don't want that either. I want them to be far away from my children's school.

So, please let me understand this. You don't want these people to remain in prison for life?

No.

And you don't want to euthanize them in order to get justice whilst making our streets safer for everyone?

No.

But you also don't want these very dangerous people to live anywhere near to you or your precious family?

Correct.

But you are more than happy for killers, rapists, home-invaders, carjackers, muggers, drug pushers, bullies, terrorists and paedophiles to be rehoused elsewhere, perhaps in areas where the vast majority of folk would vote in favour of capital punishment if offered the choice and given a referendum on the subject?

Yes, correct, exactly! I want the worst type of violent and sexual criminals to be rehabilitated and then released into someone else's neighbourhood; you know, where poor people live, somewhere like that, far away.

And if the rapists and killers and terrorists and paedophiles and drug pushers continue reoffending, destroying lives, destroying civilisation and killing and traumatising every innocent in sight, will you personally be held responsible? Will you consent to being punished due to demanding they were not only released but released in areas where there are few to no bleeding-hearted liberals or criminal sympathisers?

No, because I am exercising my democratic right to voice my opinion, that is all. I am doing the right thing, but of course I do not want everyone in my street to be a paedophile or rapist or killer.

So you support democracy and people power?

Yes, of course!

So you would approve of a referendum on capital punishment and voluntary (Opt-In) taxation?

No.

Why not?

That is different.

Is it? Or are you just a fascist, supremacist and sadomasochist who desires more pain and suffering to be caused to innocents whilst you remain protected in your enclaves and bubbles far away from the crime and disorder and societal chaos you cause by advocating in favour of psychopathic predators and the violent minority who rape, rob, kill and terrorise with impunity?

'….'

Well?

'….'

Hello?

'….'

Chapter Ten—What Would Jesus Do?

'Clowns can get away with murder.'
—John Wayne Gacy, a businessman who worked as an amateur clown and was convicted of killing thirty-three young men.

Don't waste your precious finite time pondering, 'What would Jesus do?' because he is said to be immortal, unkillable—a literal superhero.

You are flesh and blood, so when bullies come with knives or guns and demand your freedom or possessions or your family (who will be slaves for these men), ask yourself not what Jesus would do because he could (you may believe) bring back the dead and magic fish and alcohol into existence. Rather, think about what God would want you to do in that situation, with the answer presenting itself to you almost immediately:

God would not want the enemies of righteousness and grace and order and peace and civility to be victors, would He?

God does not desire for good, humble and decent folk to become slaves.

He would desire for you to rise up, fight back and stamp out the evils of slavery and servitude and unrighteousness and would turn His back on you if he saw you turning your back on your responsibilities, your duties and running away from problems rather than facing them head-on, rather than risking your life to save your precious family whom you claim to love and adore more than anything.

God does not want the bully to conquer you, meaning you must conquer and tame the bully, immediately. Do not wait a lifetime to get justice and create peaceful order; there is disorder just outside your door because we spend too much time in places of worship, too much time watching TV and destroying ourselves with idleness and addiction and obesity.

What god would smile and applaud as you agree not to fight back against four armed home invaders, which will enable them to rape your family members and relieve you of all your valuables, your pride, your honour and your soul?

A sick, evil and twisted god.

God wants you to fight back against violent bullies who threaten harm against humans and humanity and civilisation, fight back each and every time even if that makes you feel more human than elevated, peaceful and benevolent spirit; even if that makes you feel 'less Jesus-like'. You are you, just be you and crime and disorder will go down as your spirits, happiness and wealth all increase day after day.

Jesus definitely killed mosquitos and midges and other flying insects, which are referred to in the Old Testament as pests and plagues, and in the New Testament Jesus' cousin and mentor almost exclusively ate insects and Jesus spoke about livestock being 'fattened up for slaughter', him likely killing animals himself.

If God created man in the way the Old Testament claims, and if Adam or Eve killed a mosquito, would God appear and scold Adam and Eve?

No, he would say to them, 'Well done, wise humans, you have chosen life and liberty over death and slavery to another species, a lesser species. You have recognised the need to be strong, the need to protect yourself and your role as alphas, as caretakers and shepherds of this world.'

Kill the insect before it bites you or your child; this is the will of God. If you believe in God or in gods, only an evil and sadistic anti-human force (the devil) would want good folk to be endlessly bitten by mosquitos and alligators and wolves.

We have been bestowed with inner qualities and abilities that allow us to survive ice ages.

We are much stronger than we know, yet we become useless when endowed with too much privilege and not enough responsibilities and duties, it being our purpose to work and toil and struggle.

When our purpose is absent, of course we welcome being killed by the malaria-carrying mosquito or the alligator or the terrorist, bully or corrupt politician, believing we deserve it, as we reject existence when it no longer offers us challenge or excitement or opportunity for growth and glory.

Would the (Judeo-Christian) God turn his back on a human who saved his own life or his child's by keeping a leper away from his village or farm or who saved his own life and his child's by killing tens of thousands of mosquitos before the malaria-spreading destroyers of humanity had chance to exterminate his family?

No. God, in this instance, would agree that the leper had to be kept out just as the mosquitos He created had to be destroyed in order for humans to survive.

Chapter Eleven—Jesus and Christians

"You learn what you need to kill and take care of the details. It's like changing a tire. The first time you're careful. By the thirtieth time, you can't remember where you left the lug wrench."
—Ted Bundy, one of the most notorious criminals of the last twentieth century.

Despite the history of Christianity being rather blood and gore filled with occasional Crusades and witch burnings and persecution of cats and Jews, in more modern times the anti-death penalty lobby have cited Jesus and his philosophy as a reason why we should allow psychopaths to kill and rape with impunity.

Firstly, Jesus never mentioned mental illness, or psychopathy, or dinosaurs in the New Testament, there is much he did not say. Read my upcoming expansive work *The Christ Conspiracy, aka the Rise of the Light Triads* if you wish to better understand Jesus and the origins of Christianity and thus the origin of modern Western belief systems, if you have an interest in such things.

And due to Jesus never mentioning psychopaths, sociopaths, schizophrenia and much else (he only mentioned "demons", once killing a herd of someone else's pigs who were taken over by demons, apparently), Christians are given an inaccurate and skewed view of humanity, a simplistic and childlike view that 'all people are innocent and equal always no matter what', which is obviously false.

Jesus did not know about personality disorders, psychopathy, compassionate narcissism, masochism and much else as he was the son of a carpenter, rather than the son of Freud.

Those who strictly adhere to religions of any kind desire monotropistic simplicity, they desire the world explained to them in the simplest terms possible—and in regards to Christianity, there is good and evil, yet evil can become good by repenting, by apologising and being remade, with God/Jesus/Christians collectively (it seems) being benevolent, altruistic, kind, loving and tolerant and virtuous when they turn the other cheek when a serial child rapist strikes again and he is forgiven again or when the murderer is released into the community, rather than being given a lethal injection, and then goes on to kill more people.

If all people were the same, from birth, it would be possible to see every crime, act of inhumanity and misstep as a forgivable act that magically disappears the moment the offender apologises, but we are not all the same, far from it. Many among our number (between one and five percent according to most psychological studies) are incapable of experiencing empathy.

You may be squeamish about killing a serial killer or serial rapist or hard drug pusher, but these same people positively revel in hurting and killing humans. They are incapable of being rehabilitated and eat tolerant liberal Christians for breakfast.

Once upon a time, the priest or vicar or pastor demanded the people go to war, persecute cats and Jews, and hunt for "witches", yet these same folk today instead eternally call for peace and tolerance and turning the other cheek, which is severely endangering the flock whilst also leaving them vulnerable to the many predators within the clergy—covered extensively within the *Christ Conspiracy* work, which will end paedophilia within all world religions; it's time.

When our leaders and the clergy are righteous, honourable, strong and altruistic, there is no tolerance for murder, rape, paedophilia or corruption; yet when our leaders and clergy are paedophilic and corrupt as they desperately cling on to power in a new reality whereby all voters and parishioners have access to a wealth of information and opposing views and philosophies and political doctrines, of course these people ever defend the rapist, ever demand sentences are lowered as they also demand the age of consent is lowered concurrently.

Yet, beyond politics and the current abysmal state of many branches of the clergy in the world, Christian and non-Christian alike, let us look at Jesus. Let us briefly assess whether or not the 'Prince of Peace' would allow rape and murder to flourish all around him if he lived in, say, London or New York in 2024.

Jesus, many Christians insist, is God, as they insist God is Jesus, one and the same. This is why Jesus, it is claimed, was able to heal a leper, able to achieve that miracle due to him being God and thus the creator of leprosy; he was undoing his own work.

After Jesus' death, and some claim rebirth in Heaven, Jesus (Christians claim) watched on as millions of Christians for the next centuries were horribly killed by leprosy, with infectious diseases such as leprosy condemning folk in Christian Europe, for instance, to being cast out, with the Catholic Church announcing many moons ago that you were no longer considered a human being once you were stricken by leprosy, that you were the walking dead.

If Jesus was God, who could see the future, not only did he not give forewarning about the Holocaust, the genocides that would be committed against North and South American natives, the pogroms that occurred in Eastern Europe/Russia or about the AIDS epidemic and COVID, but he also knew that millions, hundreds of millions of Christians would die for a certainty as a result of typhus, cholera, plague, leprosy, malaria and dozens of other rather nasty non-man-made killers—none of the things previously listed could exist without God, without a Creator.

The philosophy attributed to Jesus speaks of forgiveness and tolerance and love for all manner of people, including for criminals and anti-civilisation forces in our midst. This is idealism, wishful thinking and naivety.

If a man is psychopathic (he doesn't know when he hurts and doesn't care if he hurts, he is driven in a predatory way to achieve pleasure and power for himself to the detriment of all others) in addition to being uneducated and narcissistic and egocentric enough never to choose to read a book of any kind, he will accept all the Christian love and forgiveness being offered whilst pretending that he is not a snake, that he is not the closest thing to evil possible.

Animals, of all kinds, experience empathy, meaning dark triads (the proven dangerous mixture of psychopathy, narcissism and Machiavellianism – which when combined births extreme individualism and sadism, aka evil, observed in many prisoners during psychological studies) should be treated as lower and less deserving than animals, with empathy being the sign of man, rather than man being defined by having opposable thumbs.

The dark triad, or the antisocial and socially destructive sociopath, will always end up stealing from the collection plate, will always spread false rumours leading to witch hunts, will always end up poisoning the Communion wine or stealing it. He will always claim to have 'Now seen the light,' will always claim to have suddenly 'been born again' when standing trial for multiple crimes against humanity. Some claim war criminals should be hung, which suggests peacetime violent criminals, who target their own tribe, should certainly be hung as their crimes and infractions were as a result of their own selfishness and inhumanity rather than following orders or due to being patriotic.

So let us put Jesus in a modern setting, London or New York (or Madrid, Paris, Rome or Tokyo).

His neighbour rapes a child.

His neighbour is incapable of ever experiencing empathy or love or fear even if he lives to be 500 years of age because he was born that way. The reality is many people are like this and when we become liberal and weak and increase the welfare state, such people are able to reproduce and reproduce and reproduce, which is akin to releasing thousands of killer snakes into the long grass where our children play. We are recklessly setting ourselves up to fail; this is extreme naivety and self-sabotage. This will not end well; there will be a price to pay for all of this virtue-signalling back-slapping tolerance.

Does Jesus desire the rapist to go to prison for fifty years knowing that will prevent many other rapes, prevent the man killing children, prevent mobs forming that will overthrow the government and cause chaos and knowing that citizens will be forced to toil for that bit longer in the fields in order to pay the extra taxes needed to fund the prison stay of the violent, predatory, non-empathic rapist snake in our midst?

Most Christians in 2024, especially those who refuse to get their houses in order as they join candlelit vigils outside US prisons demanding that the most violent, rapacious thugs are freed and forgiven, will say, 'No, Jesus would forgive him if he converted to Christianity; he would wash the man's feet and kiss his cheek.'

So, if Jesus would not consent to this danger to society pushing up everyone's taxes as a result of his lifelong incarceration, would Jesus prefer for this man, who is incapable of love, fear or any emotion, to be euthanized?

Again, most Christians in the 21st century will say, 'No, Jesus/God loves everyone, even if they are serial killers and serial child rapists.'

I disagree, strongly.

Imagine this scenario:
Jesus stops the mob killing his paedophile neighbour.

Jesus stops the police or soldiers from placing the serial child rapist (who also killed five of his victims) into prison for the remainder of his life.

Jesus then, in effect, becomes responsible for the man and it becomes Jesus' duty to protect Christian children from coming to harm as a result of his liberal and progressive, woke and tolerant views on criminals, the criminal justice system and recidivism.

Fast-forward one week.

A man and wife visit their local church in New York or London (remember, this is the second coming, Jesus is back living among us in 2024) and they are stopped by their priest before they can take their seats.

The priest asks, 'Where are your two young children?'

They reply, 'Both raped and killed; it was the unrepentant psychopathic serial paedophile rapist murderer who Jesus saved last week from the mob and from life imprisonment. We were told to have faith that tolerance and forgiveness and turning the other cheek would work, that these ideals would humble the non-empathic and narcissistic and thus inhuman dangerous snake and scourge in our midst; yet, sadly, two members of the congregation and of our family are now dead, after being terrified and hurt before their end at the hands of a monster who wishes to pervert and terrify and destroy humanity and all goodness and higher ideals and righteousness.'

Fast-forward two more weeks.

Five more couples visit the same church, all of them without their children who have been murdered by all of the psychopathic predators that Jesus has been protecting and helping.

The priest thinks to himself, *Before too long Christianity is going to die because all new Christians are being consumed and killed by non-Christian serial killers. Is this Christianity? Is this what we all deserve? Shouldn't there exist some sort of deterrent? Shouldn't we righteously fight back and defend our children before Christianity becomes abandoned due to it no longer being the shepherd that helps and protects the people, all the people, rather than just the most violent and criminal few?*

Within a few weeks there is a large march through the streets of New York City and another one through the streets of London, with all of the protestors being women holding up signs stating things such as, 'I carried and protected my baby for nine months, then he was taken away from me and the killer is protected by God. How can I pray to such a god?'

The marches were in response to the thousands upon thousands of rapes and murders of children going unpunished.

Questions.

Would Jesus stand up from his throne in Buckingham Palace or the White House or in the Empire State Building and heckle the mothers who were demanding that child killers be either incarcerated until they die or euthanized?

Would Jesus tell the protesting Christians, wounded as a result of being tolerant and forgiving and turning the other cheek and consenting to live alongside proven bad guys and proven bad girls that, 'You are worse than rapists and killers, you should return to your homes lest I become angered'?

Would Jesus threaten the protestors with hell for disagreeing with his 'one shoe fits all' simplistic philosophy that does not work in practice, which in fact only proliferates the number of sociopaths, psychopaths and dark triads in society and creates unholy things such as the Spanish Inquisition, the Crusades, pogroms against Jews and minorities and witch and cat hunts over a period of centuries?

The New Testament, mixed with some aspects of the Old Testament (picking and choosing this and that, for instance, keeping thou shalt not kill but omitting an eye for an eye), is not a good blueprint for the harmonious running of a society or nation. Many of these works are romantic, full of passion and fiction, with one of the gospels being written by an unknown author many decades after Jesus' claimed death and resurrection; we do not know who wrote the majority of the New or Old Testaments.

They are not a guide to creating a utopia, as is evidenced by the fact that when Christianity reigned supreme, when it was at its strongest in Europe and the Americas, the very worst type of abuses were made possible. For instance, the first slave ship bringing African slaves to the USA was called *The Good Ship Jesus* whose captain was fiercely Christian and insisted his crew were similarly 'good Christians': The transatlantic slave trade could not have occurred without Christianity, there are many papers and books on this subject alone.

If you travelled back 2,000 years and met Jesus and educated him in regards to psychiatry and psychology, explaining the scientifically proven facts that some people cannot be healed, that they will always be murderous and will always try to rape, rob and kill, would he still have told folk to turn the other cheek? No, I believe the answer to this question is no.

If humanity was comprised of nothing but neurotypicals, how the vast majority (90% plus) of human beings are commonly referred to, then there would be a case for turning the other cheek, forgiveness and tolerance and not having societal punishment via all the intrinsic parts of the judiciary of every nation. However, this is not the case; neurotypicals, despite being the majority, are not representative of all people, with neurotypicals being the victims most of the time, considered 'sheep' by serial killer serial rapists and the clergy alike.

Psychopaths are great for the tribe when there is a war. They are the ones who torture and kill for us, who happily get their hands dirty, who relish causing pain and suffering, yet none of their actions are patriotic, they are the beasts who we release to kill the beasts from the other side. However, when we have won a hard-fought peace, these killers and destroyers of virtue and goodness and civilisation become ever-present dangers unless we have the strength and courage enough to keep them down, under control and at our mercy, rather than us being at theirs.

Freeing rapists and killers makes Christians feel good but endangers their children and the children of non-Christians, is that what Jesus and God want? No, that would be absurd.

If a dog kills a baby, the dog is euthanized; so too, more so in fact, should this be the case when a human kills a baby. The dog didn't know any better, the dog is not a Homo sapien; it may have been hungry or thought it needed to protect itself, whereas a rapist or a murderer (in a premeditated, deliberate murder) or a hard drug pusher knows exactly what they are doing, and you do not come back from such actions and atrocities. Even if you say you have changed, you remain the same beast who was capable of inhumanity, who was lacking in empathy, who will always be lacking in empathy, compassion and love.

Christians, some at least, want to 'save everyone', why?

Because they wish to be saved themselves and to create balance due to feeling bad or guilty for things they have done in their lives. We all commit infractions or sins of some sort or another, be it angrily shouting at a fellow motorist and wishing him dead, gossiping and spreading rumours or stealing or not paying taxes, which makes good people feel guilty and uncomfortable afterwards, as good people (the majority) desire to follow the rules, create cohesion and peace and be good children, good citizens and good souls.

The same Christians who are on personal journeys with their faith and belief system need to understand something of fundamental importance:

1/ You are not Jesus and to try to mimic him is in bad taste and rather than being flattery is more like heresy or blasphemy and

2/ It is not possible to save everyone as a minority of our number only desire to hurt, rape, sully, degrade, demoralise and kill.

It makes us feel good when we help others, especially narcissists, who get a special thrill and sense of supremacy and high virtue when they help a blind man cross a road or fund the lifestyle of heroin addicts by giving them a twenty-pound or twenty-dollar note. Oh, so virtuous and amazing, so Jesus-like....

And the ultimate act of benevolence and altruism and self-abnegation is of course to release a lion in a small community where it will kill and kill and kill and kill and kill and kill and kill and kill all of the self-hating Christians and their innocent children. Murderous psychopaths in prison awaiting execution are unempathic, murderous lions; the fact that they look human is irrelevant.

If Christians wish to hate themselves, that is fine, although this saddens me because life is short and we should all desire more happiness than sadness, more standing than kneeling, more bravery than meek surrender and servitude. It is every man and woman's right to hate themselves and give away their finite resources to baby killers if that is their 'thing', if that makes them feel better about Jesus allegedly being killed; yet when their actions, such as candlelit vigils that are an attempt at introducing murderous rapists into the communities where their children play and frolic, they have gone too far, far too far, and all because they are upset by the pending execution.

They do not wish to witness death, they do not wish for the euthanasia to be carried out in their name and they are willing to gamble with the lives of their children if need be in order to prevent state-sanctioned executions, but they will never try to stop individual sociopaths or psychopaths from continuing their murder sprees.

Christians, love your children and protect them by keeping the snakes and wolves at bay, and this is only possible if you are willing to get uncomfortable, willing to get blood on your hands. God will not hate you for saving your Christian child by doing the right thing; He will love you for it, He will consider you a responsible parent and dutiful shepherd, rather than a weakling and lamb to the slaughter.

Chapter Twelve—Euthanasia for Lifelong Dangerous Criminals (Who Cannot Be/Refuse to Be Rehabilitated) Is Humane

'I didn't relate to Sharon Tate as being anything but a store mannequin ... [she] sounded just like an IBM machine ... She kept begging and pleading and pleading and begging [for the life of her unborn child], and I got sick of listening to her, so I stabbed her.'

—Susan Atkins, who confessed to her crimes, including the murder of pregnant actress Sharon Tate.

Keeping a man or woman in prison for life is of course extremely costly, traumatic for the individual and traumatic for the individual's relatives and friends whilst being unethical in terms of forcing victims to pay (via taxes) to feed, clothe and house the offenders who destroyed their lives.

Lifelong imprisonment is a living death, with hope gone and no chance for freedom because certain violent offenders will never change because one cannot change genetics or DNA. Every attempt has been made for untold thousands of years to change people, yet every attempt, including the administering of drugs, is fruitless. Killers will kill, rapists will rape, paedophiles will continue harming your children and corrupt politicians will continue being corrupt until they fear being executed as a consequence of their corruption and treason.

Yet, beyond the costs to the taxpayers and the emotional costs to the relatives and friends of the imprisoned offender, the argument should be made that it is inhumane to keep any man or woman behind bars for the entirety of their lives as living in chains, living behind bars, is worse than death, most would agree.

The rates of reoffending (recidivism) are troubling in modern neoliberal Western nations. Everything that has been attempted has failed; the only tried and tested method to prevent murderers, paedophiles and terrorists from reoffending is capital punishment.

The only way to prevent a serial killer continuing to destroy the lives of dozens and dozens of families (each murder destroys the lives of many people whilst also spreading fear and trauma throughout the community) is to end the serial killer's life—and all serial killers, of course, start out by killing a single innocent human.

Those who advocate that there should not be capital punishment also desire to release from custody the most violent and unrepentant killers as early as possible. Tell an anti-death penalty advocate that a man who raped and brutally murdered a one-year-old baby has been sentenced to thirty years in prison with no chance of early release or parole and that he must break rocks for thirty years whilst in custody and they will march, protest, even riot to get "justice" for the monster who only looks human on the outside. Inside there exists pure evil.

This is why such folk as this need to be ignored as they ignore the plight of the victims' relatives; they only desire to save and comfort and liberate the very worst of us.

When they succeed, when the baby killer is released, will he rape and kill again?

If he gets the opportunity, yes of course he will, unless taxes rise exponentially and he is under surveillance 24/7 for the remainder of his life as all good people everywhere hold their breath waiting for the inevitable to occur. And when it occurs, the liberal defenders of the criminal are nowhere to be found. They will hide away when the man they freed rapes or kills again, ever is it so.

Chapter Thirteen—The 'Push the Button' Scenario

'After my head has been chopped off, will I still be able to hear, at least for a moment, the sound of my own blood gushing from my neck? That would be the best pleasure to end all pleasure.'

—Peter Kürten (before placing his head into the guillotine at his execution. Kürten was a German serial killer, also known as the 'Vampire of Düsseldorf.' He was convicted of nine counts of murder.

You will never be punished if you push the button, no one will ever know if you push this button, and if you believe in a god or gods, they fully approve of your actions in this scenario, so long as you push the button; but you need to make a choice.

Pushing the button in front of you in this very moment will prevent one million rapes from occurring this year, will prevent new cases of paedophilia and murder and hate and disorder and PTSD from occurring this year and prevent massive rises in taxes occurring this year to pay for violent predators (who often are devoid of empathy completely and have no remorse whatsoever and are keen to hurriedly reoffend again and again) to be housed in prisons and thereafter given welfare and free housing and free healthcare for the remainder of their very long taxpayer-funded lives.

If you push the button, it will mean that the very moment a criminal attempts to commit a violent crime, rape, paedophilia, murder, terrorism or an act of political corruption/treason, a home invasion, a mugging, a carjacking, or the moment a man tries to sell fentanyl to a ten-year-old child, each and every one of these offenders will have a sudden heart attack—and ten seconds later, they will fall down, never to stand again.

If you don't push the button, because of your morals or your virtues or exalted principles and ideology, you knowingly, in effect, kill thousands of innocents and cause millions to be raped and you are the cause of pain and suffering everywhere, all so you can feel a little better about yourself. You say, 'Who am I to judge? Who am I to interfere? Why should I stop crime? Why should I prevent suffering?' You are lost to this cult. You need to read every book in this series if you would not push the button. Those who love humanity would choose to end violent and sexual and traumatising crime/unrighteousness when given the opportunity.

Juries and judges have long chosen to push the button when the destroyers of humanity and civilisation find themselves in court charged with the most heinous crimes. They did their duty for their species and for civilisation despite it not being easy for good people, for innocents, to be responsible for a man's or woman's death—yet, consistently, evil-doers were executed by the people in every nation due to the self-sacrifice and altruism and love of normal, regular folk who never wanted to kill, never wanted to harm a hair on a serial rapist's or serial killer's head but the need for them to do so far outweighed their individual positions on crime and punishment and capital punishment.

When the tribe and community need heroes, honourable and peaceful and good folk will become mighty towers of stoicism as they push that button without a glimmer of happiness or joy on their faces as ending the lives of even the most barbarous and soulless individuals is a sombre and serious affair. It is not about revenge, not about pleasure, not about hate but a deterrent and justice and a way to ensure order and community returns as law-abiding and honest folk are protected and loved, rather than excessive love being granted to the self-loving narcissist rapist and paedophile and pleasure-seeking serial killer.

The needs of the many far outweigh the needs of rapists, terrorists, paedophiles killers, corrupt politicians, bullies and gangsters.

So, did you push the button?

If you did, you must desire capital punishment and you must push your representatives to introduce it or to hold a referendum on the subject. Thank you for pushing the button, it means a lot; it means humanity has not yet surrendered, that the spirit of man is still strong!

However, if you did not push the button, if 'feeling good' inside, if your feelings and conscience are more important to you than ending all avoidable suffering and pain and misery, please place a large sign in your window, in your garden, on your vehicle and another around your neck immediately (if you wish to be honest, rather than a hypocrite) stating:

'I tolerate sex crimes and corruption and violence and living in fear. Look at me, everybody, I am a victim. If you punch me I will not punch you back; if you are a violent thief and bully and rapist, look here, in my direction, because I am a willing sacrifice and masochist and fool.'

Chapter Fourteen—Cognitive Dissonance

'That is my ambition, to have killed more people—more helpless people—than any man or woman who has ever lived.'
—Jane Toppan, who admitted to killing at least thirty-one people.

Being anti-capital punishment (saving the lives of terrorists and rapists and murderers and paedophiles and corrupt and treasonous politicians when the people demand they be hung) requires deep cognitive dissonance, which is evidenced below:

Is there really enough evidence?
Was it a first offence?
He has served his community for many years in the capacity of teacher or police officer or priest or business owner or volunteer fire-fighter.
It will make people scared if someone is killed, even if that someone is an unrepentant, evil predator who will destroy all of humanity if given the means and opportunity to do so.
Doesn't he have a family?
Doesn't he/she have dependants?
He only raped/killed a few people.
What if the confession is fake?
What if he has the mental age of a child?
What if he regrets what he did and has "found religion"?
Isn't he a veteran? Isn't he a former sheriff? Isn't he a celebrity? Can't we 'cut him some slack'?
What if the victim "deserved it"?
What if … what if … what if… what if….

Let us dispense with this nonsense and bleeding-heartedness and misplaced loyalty, which blinds folk, which clouds the debate, and, yes, there is a debate.
There must be a debate on this issue, everywhere—and if you would not insist that your son or husband be executed for rape/murder, what you effectively are saying to their victims during the rape/murder is, 'Do NOT resist, my family deserves to have power over you. Do not attempt to kill your rapist or would-be murderer because they are related to me. Your rights and life do not matter; only my family matters, only our lives matter.'

Do not be this way, never think this way. Never get angry when your relative is executed for a string of rapes or murders or for being a home-invading terrorist or a religious terrorist or a corrupt politician or a corrupt cop—because dangerous criminals need to be disowned and removed from society completely.

Let us approach the removal of elements of society that will destroy society for a certainty, given enough tolerance and time and forgiveness and liberalism, without the multiple emotional inane excuses and justifications for extending the lives of the predators and human haters and civilisation haters in our midst. Let us begin the debate at the following point:

All excuses are deemed to be irrelevant and the criteria, the very strict criteria anti-capital punishment advocates have introduced, have all been met. Confession – yes, perfect evidence – yes; every single man and woman in the nation knows and believes the defendant is guilty of the crimes in question, as it is in the vast majority of cases. Let this be the starting point.

Now let us debate; should the many pay more tax to enable the life-extension of clear and present dangers to them who have been found guilty to everyone's satisfaction? Should we be bankrupted by extending the lives of terrorists, paedophiles and unrepentant violent thugs and gangsters?

Chapter Fifteen—Capital Punishment Categories

'I tried to create living zombies with uric acid in the drill [to the head], but it never worked. I just wanted to have the person under my complete control, not having to consider their wishes, being able to keep them there as long as I wanted.'
—Jeffrey Dahmer, the 'Milwaukee Cannibal', convicted of the rape, murder and dismemberment of sixteen men and boys. Many of his later murders involved necrophilia, cannibalism, and the preservation of body parts of his victims.

If good, innocent and hardworking people desire to live safely, if good people desire to pay the lowest taxes possible, and if harmony, rather than chaos and fear, is desired, these are the categories of people who should be euthanized following a lawful trial:

Rapists/Attempted Rapists
Murderers/Attempted Murderers
Terrorists/Attempted Terrorists
Paedophiles
Treasonous, Nepotistic or Corrupt Politicians and Representatives
Treasonous, Nepotistic or Corrupt Public Servants
Home Invaders/Burglars
Violent Criminals – muggers, carjackers, those who use weapons/threats of violence
CEOs/Business People who knowingly poison consumers and the planet
Drug Dealers/Drug Pushers
Repeat Offenders (sex crimes/terrorism/violent crime)
Psychological Abusers/Antisocial Torturers
Domestic Abusers and Animal Abusers who emotionally, psychologically or physically sadistically bully and abuse innocents

<u>An overview as to why each category of people above needs to be removed from society completely, immediately:</u>

First, it is important to understand that some commit crime out of necessity (poverty/being low-functioning), some commit crime for a thrill or to get attention or even to alleviate boredom, some commit crime to feed self-destructive habits/addictions, others enjoy the 'risk' of committing crime (think kleptomania), while others commit crime for reasons of sadism, pleasure and self-gratification . Only children and the uneducated or deliberately blinkered think every criminal/prisoner the same; we are all fundamentally different:

Is the man who steals bread to feed his family the same as the man who steals TVs and cars to fund his drug addiction? And is that man the same as the serial killer who stalks and murders women after brutally torturing them? No, ergo—we are all different. Convicted traitors, paedophiles and serial killers deserve no rights, no freedoms, no state protection; these enemies of the people cannot be even thought of as being people, certainly not showered in welfare and healthcare and love.

In prisons across the world, the majority of offenders found therein are, for the most part, sociopathic, psychopathic, sadistic and lacking in empathy in general. Some are born different (in the case of psychopaths and schizophrenics) whereas others, due to bad nurture, have come to be different as in the case of the sociopathic minority and those with antisocial personality disorders.

When I talk about ending a man's (or woman's) life due to him/her committing crimes and unrighteous and inhuman actions against innocents, which will eventually destroy the entire civilisation, I do not think in terms of classes, as in 'Poor people who commit crime because they have no stake in society should be put to death.' No, the opposite is true, with those most deserving of being removed from society and existence being CEOs who psychopathically choose more millions or billions for themselves whilst knowingly killing their customers whilst ushering in an inglorious and base culture.

The law and the death sentence, historically in many places, have served to protect the poor, as is evidenced in the case of the inscription on the Old Bailey in London, the high court of the UK: 'Defend the children of the poor and punish the wrongdoer.' What a beautiful and motivating and loving statement. Yet, in this neoliberal woke era of decline, failure, obesity, deprivation, poverty, mass rapes, mass crime and mass debt and mass apathy, there is seemingly no 'wrongdoer' any more, just excuses for repeated bad and toxic behaviour—'He had a hard life,' 'She had a hard life,' etc. No more excuses; there is right and there is wrong and there will be justice and peace.

Paedophiles

If there is a man or a woman who is attracted to a six-month-old baby, that person needs to be removed from the community for the remainder of their life and if a minority of vocal folk are too squeamish to desire for that individual to have a tattoo or brand put upon their forehead declaring, 'Danger to children,' the man or woman attracted to babies needs to be legally removed from existence or kept, housed, fed, taken care of, nurtured and protected for the remainder of their lives by woke liberal saviours and woke liberal saviours only.

The era of folk who desire capital punishment for dangerous criminal forces in our midst being compelled to pay for food, medicine, healthcare and housing for the very worst of us must come to an end immediately. This madness has lasted far too long. How is it fair that victims of rape are forced to pay to house and feed their rapist in prison? How is this fair or reasonable? How is this "progressive"? This is sick, unconscionable and cruel.

If woke liberals desire to fund the lifestyle and housing and healthcare of paedophiles, they should be free to do so, yet the vast majority of normal and healthy-minded folk who are not bleeding-hearted, who do not have any sympathy for those sexually attracted to children or babies should not be forced to pay a single cent or penny to keep alive the worst type of predator and threat to their precious children and the precious children of their friends and loved ones.

First offence = death penalty. If you were shipwrecked on a desert island with just your three young children and a paedophile, your mind would work correctly, as nature/God intended.

So, for instance, when the paedophile (anti-human, non-empathic monster who hates you and who is irredeemable) assaulted your eldest child, say he or she was six years of age, you would never tolerate this action and turn the other cheek. You would never choose to gamble with the safety and lives of your children; you would never sacrifice your child on the altar of woke, pacifist, progressive neo-liberalism, would you?

For a certainty, to prevent pain and trauma and indignity and terror being inflicted on your young ones, who needed you, who saw you as their god, their protector, their shepherd, their everything, you would find a rock or tree branch and bludgeon the evil predator to death as the only other course of action would be to become a passive fool who placed their hands over their ears and closed their eyes as they tolerated all of their offspring being abused and debased by the monster in your midst, who only appeared to be human. He or she would appear in human form, yes, but would be far from being a Homo sapien, far from being a wise man.

Your choices would be to gamble with the lives and health of your children, execute the danger to your children or imprison the paedophile threat until your children became adults and thus capable of defending themselves from sexual predators. All adults should attempt to defend themselves fully and, if necessary, to ensure they are protected, end the life even of those who attempt to rape, rob or kill them or their loved ones. This is a patriotic duty; those who do not fight back strenuously in a righteous and passionate manner, throwing everything they have at the attacker or attackers, is an accomplice to the crime. They are aiding the inhuman forces. Always fight back!

If you choose to do nothing and are tolerant and forgiving and loving (a great set of ideals in principle) all of your children will be raped and it will be your fault.

If you imprison the threat, you will be spending years, perhaps decades, sharing your resources with the criminal and dangerous element, reducing your resources and the time you can spend building, hunting, creating and trying to escape the island as you spend your time building jails, rather than building signal fires, boats or huge SOS signs on beaches.

If you execute the attacker and threat, your children are eternally safeguarded, you can use all your time and resources to escape or to make your lives as comfortable and happy as possible and you will never need to live in fear and anxiety of one day falling and breaking your leg, for instance, as you climb trees to harvest coconuts to feed the paedophile you keep locked up in a cave with bamboo bars placed at the front—because if you become injured and cannot gather food for the prisoner, your kindness for him, your compassion for him and your love for him and reluctance to be responsible and dutiful and strong will mean you will have to free him and watch on as he becomes king of the island and you become one of his several slaves.

Rapists/Attempted Rapists

The continuing existence of rape proves how apathetic and weak the majority have become, how passive and masochistic people have become.

The connection between the rise of liberalism and tolerance and the sky-rocketing numbers of reported rapes is profound, as evidenced elsewhere within this work.

When there is zero tolerance for rape, guess what. Rape decreases, massively, until it near enough disappears because a rapist desires pleasure, not public humiliation followed by a public execution.

Does your government encourage you to kill attempted rapists who attack you?

Does your school encourage you to kill attempted rapists who attack you?

Does your church or place of worship encourage you to kill attempted rapists who attack you?

The answers are likely no, no, no; which is why the number of reported rapes in places such as the UK has DOUBLED since capital punishment was shelved. No one is surprised, no one, and rapists are laughing at the tolerant liberals who willingly sacrificed millions of women, men and young boys and girls by removing the threat of the rope. Shame on those people, those abject fools. Your consciences are not clean; they are drenched in the blood and tears of millions of debased and traumatised victims.

Every prime minister, president, king and queen in every land, if they care about their people, should deliver a speech upon the occasion of them coming to represent or coming to rule over the land and people. 'I instruct each and every man, woman and child to fight to the death if ever attacked by a paedophile, rapist, violent mugger, home invader, terrorist or foreign invader wearing the uniform of another state, to fight to the death, to die on your feet!'

Who thinks incidents of rape and terrorism and paedophilia would increase after your representatives/leaders delivered that empowering speech? No one.

Yet, liberal woke folk will call me wrong, evil, perhaps even a fascist for calling for people to stand up for themselves, saying absurd things such as, 'But what if the rapist had a tough upbringing? What if he has the mental age of a child? What if the violent carjacker is a drug addict? What if the paedophile was a victim of paedophilia himself?'

The alternative to fighting back is to lie on the ground and do nothing—this is woke, progressive tolerance in an inglorious, depressing nutshell.

'Don't hurt the rapist because he has feelings, he is misunderstood, he has problems, he is a person too. Allow him to hurt you.'

What a trash philosophy and way of life this is, absolute trash.

<u>We are lions</u>, we should act like it. Do woke, neoliberal parents tell their children to try to give rapists and paedophiles therapy during a sexual assault instead of punches and pens and pencils stabbed into the attacker's eyes and throat? Yes, likely they do, which makes them unfit to be parents, voters or influencers of any kind.

Murderers/Attempted Murderers

'An eye for an eye' is an oversimplification, yet that ancient reasoning and philosophy is indeed apt and when in place massively reduces the number of premeditated murders.

The goal of capital punishment being put to the people in the form of a referendum and latterly being an accepted and established part of law and order, this information being relayed to all in school, in the home and at every stage of their lives, is not to kill people—no, of course not. Capital punishment exists to END killing, to end violence, to remove fear and terror and to empower and ennoble all law-abiding and peace-loving humans.

If you say, 'I would not want my killer to be executed, even if he/she stalked me at night and killed me solely for reasons of their own sadistic pleasure and to increase their power,' you may be happy to fully forgive the killer, who will likely go on killing and killing until finally stopped by the rope, bullet or blade; but your friends and family members are not so likely to want your killer to live a nice and comfortable and long life full of good memories and relaxation and laughter and joy. And if your will decrees that any man or woman who kills you should be pardoned and not punished, if you really are that masochistic, how will it not be your direct fault, from beyond the grave, if the killer then mass-murders your entire family? Of course your pacifism and masochism and self-abnegating, suicidal philosophy will be to blame for all the new deaths.

You may say, 'I would not want my killer to be released, not right away at least; he or she would need help and re-education first.'

To which I say, 'Why do you care about your killer when this person has just devastated your entire family, shaken your community and deeply saddened your friends and colleagues and peers? Shouldn't you focus your care and attention and empathy and love in a better direction? What if the killer is unrepentant, arrogant, belligerent, or happy about murdering an innocent?'

'But still I don't want them to be euthanized; I want people to pay taxes to keep my killer locked away safely in prison.'

I ask, 'Forever? Even with the latest technological breakthroughs and marvels, which may cause your killer to outlive you by over 100 years? So if your killer was twenty-two when he ended your life, and he lived to be 122 in prison (highly likely due to the absence of forced manual labour in most prisons) that would mean that in order for him to have enjoyed living all those extra many years, all he needed to do was stab you in the back as you walked home from work, heading home to see your wife and young child, isn't that right?'

'It would be inhumane to keep the killer locked away for 100 years though.'

'How many years would be enough then?'

'I don't know, maybe five? Maybe ten? He would need to know it is bad behaviour; maybe three years would be enough and then five years on probation.'

'And if the killer spends such little time in jail and such little on probation after, who is paying for those costs and his legal aid and for the trial and his rehousing and his likely new identity and potentially welfare for the remainder of his life?'

'Taxpayers.'

'Even those who want capital punishment to return?'

'Yes.'

'Why?'

'Because if only the people like me, who are against capital punishment, are forced to pay tax for prisons, we will be paying a 90% tax rate, that is why.'

'And do you think that it is fair or democratic to force everyone to fund life-extensions of killers and terrorists and paedophiles and traitors when the majority want all of these people to be euthanized immediately?'

'….'

***

Of course there will always be leeway and extenuating circumstances in regards to certain cases of murder/manslaughter, with self-defence never warranting capital punishment, with a man defending his home or nation who is forced to kill the invader never needing to worry about the rope or guillotine. All know of the types and categories of folk who will fear capital punishment when they commit murder. It is the gangsters; it is the known violent criminals; it is the men and women of previous bad character; it is assassins; it is bullies; it is criminals being prevented from getting their way who resort to murder to steal or to escape. No innocent man or woman need fear the rope; only the wrongdoer is kept awake at night when capital punishment is reintroduced.

Terrorists/Attempted Terrorists

If the terrorist loves your nation and wishes to "liberate her" or hates your nation and wishes to dominate her, either way that individual needs to be hurriedly legally euthanized if they resort to violent tactics, especially when innocents are targeted in a deliberate attempt to scare all people everywhere in order to spread fear.

I am not afraid, nor should you be, and there are many who are equally unafraid and will not be cowed by cowardly bullying tactics such as these. There are many among us who would instantly throw ourselves at terrorists armed with whatever we could find in that moment seeking to prevent them achieving their inglorious goals.

We saw this in London some years back when a lone hero stood up to murderous terrorists who were targeting innocent civilians; we observed this also in Scotland some years back at an airport. We see this everywhere and we will continue to see strong men and women rising and standing up to wrongdoers because humanity refuses to be enslaved. We refuse to be bullied and we demand that peace, righteousness and civilisation reign supreme, forever.

If civilians and the police are not able to euthanize the terrorist, he or she will go on to cost the taxpayer somewhere in the region of $10M in their lives. This is a reward, a reward for being a murderous thug fuelled by a doctrine of hate who desired to dominate and bully and get what they wanted. If they truly hate your nation, they will relish bankrupting you in this way. They will delight in launching fruitless appeals, further draining your resources and your sanity as taxpayers will cover all the costs. The only ones who benefit? Terrorists and lawyers.

There will be expensive trials; there will be an expensive lengthy prison sentence; there will be a prolonged probation period following release; there will be intelligence agents from the government being paid for decades to 'keep tabs' on the terrorist, and there will be unending amounts of legal aid paid to the terrorist as they attempt to use our good laws and civility and decency against us whilst laughing as the treasury is emptied in order to fund the lifestyles of hundreds and then thousands and then tens of thousands of terrorists, attempted terrorists, terrorist sympathisers and supporters.

In this era of CCTV, DNA, GPS and smartphone cameras, we know the man or woman is guilty within seconds. There is no need for a trial oftentimes, not a lengthy trial at least, for instance in the case of terror attacks in Central London captured on hundreds of CCTV cameras in which the defendants admitted guilt immediately. They were captured surrendering to police on their bodycams because the cowards did not fight to the death, because they wanted to live, which is the only reason the terror attack occurred—because the UK does not have capital punishment in place for acts of terror against the people, but it should. Hospital care and treatment for terrorists is unnecessary. Terrorists should be euthanized immediately, via a rope—will this create one million new terrorists?

No, it will end terrorism. He/she will be hung with the same rope that paedophiles and home invaders and treasonous politicians are hung with. They are all the same kettle of fish, reuse the rope.

If you know for a fact that the very worst thing that will happen to you if you start a stabbing spree in your local town or city centre, killing seven children and fifteen adults, some in wheelchairs, is a paid vacation in prison where you will get three good meals per day, free dental treatment, free heating, free television, and free hot water and thereafter you will be given a free house and a new identity and free money for the remainder of your natural life, will you be terrified of picking up the knife?

Will you be demotivated from picking up the knife and venting your anger and rage upon the majority?

No, you will more easily become a terrorist if you know the punishment is actually a reward:

Notoriety/'Cred'.

Free prison accommodation in a protected area of the prison.

Free post-prison accommodation for life.

Free money for life because few wish to employ violent criminals and no one, absolutely no one, wishes to employ convicted terrorists who have murdered children and old folk with their bare hands.

If you have to kill to achieve your goals, you have already lost. We will not be bullied and intimidated, no one is afraid. All good men stand ready and willing to become martyrs when the violent minority-rule-desiring few next take to the streets.

Treasonous, Nepotistic or Corrupt Politicians, Representatives and Public Servants

If after the introduction of capital punishment you abuse your position of temporary privilege, power and trust, you should hurriedly flee abroad as soon as possible, self-deporting yourself, going into voluntary lifelong exile if any part of you is honourable, wise or forward-looking. Knowing our collective history (which always repeats itself, always), knowing that revolutions happen at the most unexpected points in time, if you are smart and feel guilt or shame for betraying the people, go—go now, retire, remove yourself from the community you have wronged and sullied.

Like all categories of folk who should be removed from society via the swift and virtually free means of capital punishment, treasonous and corrupt politicians should not be executed tomorrow for a crime they committed many years prior—I would not enjoy the job of executioner; yet I and many others would happily, without payment, pull the lever 10,000 times if called upon to do so.

If capital punishment were to be reintroduced, it would be assumed by the majority that it would only apply to new offences because witch hunts are toxic and those who have previously dipped their snouts in the trough, who have enthusiastically been corrupt, as well as those who were 'taken along for the ride' and who feared being blacklisted if they remained clean and honest and innocent would perhaps be among your best allies when it came to ensuring that, moving forward, no more political corruption or misconduct in public office, in any public office, was possible.

Those who are the most corrupt would likely slip out of the nation on the eve of the introduction of capital punishment or be the ones most vocally opposed to a referendum being held on the issue of capital punishment, watch this space.

Whilst political corruption and nepotism and sleaze from the past can be overlooked, treason cannot; nor can it be tolerated in any fashion in the future. It must be dealt with decisively. If a public servant aids a competitor nation, sells secrets, betrays the homeland they need to be euthanized before the weekend. Failure to do so will embolden the competitor nation and before long your nation will be imperilled, your entire political system owned by the competitor, your news media owned by the competitor, and your competitor will also have huge financial influence in your land as he buys influence and causes toxic, divisive infighting whilst surpassing you in every manner, likely due to the competitor nation having capital punishment in place for treason.

Home Invaders/Burglars

What is the difference between a man from the next village or town smashing your windows, threatening you with a weapon, terrifying you almost to death, torturing you and taking from you your freedom, your possessions, your pride and your ability to control who enters your land and property and an invader from 10,000 miles away who salutes a different flag?

The answer is there is very little difference, with a home invader being an invader, an enemy, not a patriot, not a defender, not a lover of the community or the nation or civilisation—he or she is a person in chaos who seeks to spread chaos, fear and injustice. He or she is the enemy and they need to be stopped, in order for the most vulnerable folk in our communities to be able to feel safe once again, safe, proud and confident, rather than brow-beaten, petrified and depressed as they hide behind alarm systems, triple glazing, bars on windows and ten locks on every door. What kind of life is this? Is this the progressive tolerant dream? It stinks, it's trash; reject it.

If anything, the home-grown violent burglar is worse than the man following his state's orders when he invades your sovereign nation because he was raised among us, he should know better, so when he puts his foot on our throats it is the bitterest pill to swallow. The home-grown criminal, the snake, the viper in our midst is more deserving of justice and punishment than the foreign invader merely following orders. Your neighbour who smashes your window and enters your home with his four masked friends, the bullies and cowards coming in large numbers armed with weapons, should be executed as soon as possible in order to restore confidence and strength and optimism in the community, to immediately reduce the number of those lost to alcoholism, gambling, smoking and drug addictions; why a delay? Why keep alive elements that will continue raping society and spreading fear and terror?

Parents must become more responsible; communities must become more responsible; we all must become more active in how society runs and functions lest we continue being victims again and again and again. Poverty is no excuse as most poor folk would never hurt a fly. Bad education, bad role models and selfish individualism enabled by hedonistic woke liberalism and consumerism is the problem; class envy is the problem; refusing to work hard, refusing to progress up ladders and refusing to earn your food, earn your house and earn everything that comes to you is the problem.

We must remove entitlement and want, we must expose our young people only to good influences and good role models, we must no longer be dependent upon credit and we must start living within our own means as we move away from the toxic culture of keeping up with the Joneses. We can be united whilst being ourselves, separate and unique individuals who each have valuable contributions to make to the community and society. We are not all the same, so it will only cause harm and confusion if we conduct ourselves as though we were all the same.

<u>Violent Criminals – muggers, carjackers, those who use weapons/threats of violence</u>

If a violent mammal of any kind or stripe seeks to attack me, that violent mammal shall be killed within a matter of seconds, and I care not if he or she is wearing clothes or covered in fur or scales or whatever. Those who do not fight back against predators and uncivilised violent forces are slaves, which is why I always sleep with a smile on my face, just as I always smile even when threatened by antisocial criminal elements, because I am always ready to die for freedom and liberty, and so should you be, which means being always ready to prevent crime, barbarism and unrighteousness, whatever it takes, whatever the personal cost or sacrifice.

If we should 'Fight *them* on the beaches' (a foreign invader), why should we not fight *them* in our bedrooms, gardens and in our communities?

The second we stop running, the second we clench our fists, the second we fight back, every wrongdoer shall bow and beg for mercy.

Becoming a victim the majority of time requires consent; I do not give consent. I choose my own death or the death of the invader every single time rather than enrich the society-and-humanity-and-civilisation-hating bullies in our midst.

No retreat, no concessions, no tolerance for home invaders or external invaders. Do not give an inch of land, do not give a single penny; fight for what you have earned by your high endeavours and righteousness and honesty and strength and sacrifices.

Humble the attackers, defeat the attackers and make it known that your home is your fortress, which you will defend with every fibre of your being.

This is how you defeat depression and pessimism and apathy, this is how we return to glory; this is how we save our communities. This is how we will end home invasions, fear, mistrust and the collapse of civilisation.

CEOs/Business People Who Knowingly Poison Consumers

Ask me how to (unethically) make one billion dollars in the shortest space of time possible, within say twelve months, and I will respond, 'Simple. First, purchase a great quantity of an addictive substance that should never be given to children, such as nicotine, Xanax or cocaine or large amounts of caffeine. Second, lace children's sweets (candy) or cereal with the same highly addictive product. Third, sit back and watch as children insist to their parents that their favourite packet of sweets or their cereal, which is suddenly loved and adored by children far and wide, is 'my candy and cereal.'

Once the workers in the factory have gone home, no one will notice me pouring in the very addictive and stimulating additional substance, none will be the wiser. Of course children will prefer my products over my competitors' products because of the drugs included at no extra charge, meaning profits, profits, profits.

If you discovered that your children were being positioned in this way and turned into drug addicts (I mean in addition to being addicted to sugar and sodium and junk food and screens and 'content' as is depressingly the case in many places in 2024) how would you react?

Would you be apathetic and do nothing?

Would you write a strongly worded letter of complaint?

Would you simply purchase other products for your child and just hope that the new food is not manufactured by a psychopathic and very cunning and greedy Machiavellian businessman who hates children, who hates humans, who is solely driven by gold?

Or would you get off your knees and demand a referendum on capital punishment? Would you insist that, henceforth, every businessman/CEO found guilty of knowingly poisoning the people will face the prospect of capital punishment following a legal trial?

If I poison one man, my neighbour, and he dies, I will spend twenty years in prison in liberal Western nations.

Yet, if because of my greed I poison one million men, who afterwards all die or become very ill, I will donate to politicians and their parties; I will grease a few palms, pay people off, threaten other people, and not spend a single second locked up behind bars.

Including the caveat within the capital punishment framework that CEOs/business people must be euthanized if they endanger the health of millions is absolutely essential because unless there exists a deterrent, unscrupulous, unethical folk will bend the rules, break them altogether, and visit factories after midnight to add all sorts of things to your children's food, perhaps even to baby food or pharmaceutical products.

Adding CEOs to the list ensures democracy and free enterprise can continue to exist in a world made sane again by capital punishment and voluntary taxation. The last thing anyone should desire in Western capitalist states is for the state to take ownership of the running and thus responsibility for currently privately owned businesses both small and large. This is far from being a necessary step, so long as folk all play by the rules, refrain from buying influence (I cover that topic at length within my *Trump-Harris Co-Presidency* book) and are happy to compete fairly, rather than resorting to lacing children's food with cocaine and nicotine and caffeine and such like in addition to the already very unnecessary sugar that is infused into almost everything processed these days, which is perhaps the worst drug of all when one considers the obesity epidemic it helps worsen.

If profit comes before the health of the people and nation, if a deliberate decision is ever made that endangers the health of the people and nation, of course a serious crime has been committed and of course there must be consequences.

Drug Dealers/Drug Pushers

In gauging what punishment is right and just for he who sells fentanyl to an eleven-year-old boy or meth to a forty-year-old woman, we need to imagine what our communities would be like without these drugs being available whatsoever, without the frontline drug pusher, who does not casually wait for new customers to approach him but rather hunts for the most vulnerable people, the most impressionable people, even offering free samples at first to 'get them hooked'.

Without hard drugs being in the community the sun would begin shining more brightly suddenly. Apathy and depression would massively reduce; fear and anxiety would fall by the wayside; home invasions would near end; security bars would begin being removed from windows; the children's park would be filled with children again now the drug abusers and drug dealers would no longer be there—and antisocial behaviour, begging, general violence and disorder would all disappear. Everyone at every level in the community would report that they were feeling happy and free again, liberated and blessed and renewed and uplifted.

Most would agree with this assessment if they have lived in communities laid low by drug gangs, drug dealers and mass drug addiction to substances that change you, that break you, that relieve you of your sanity and free will, that compel you to steal from your own grandmother, to throw her down a flight of stairs even if she refuses to hand over her pension to you.

So, from this starting point, it is possible to know the damage drug pushers/importers/smugglers cause to every community.

They are ultimately responsible for a myriad of miseries; it all starts with them, which is why adverts for cigarettes are now forbidden in nations such as the UK and the USA due to it being cigarette adverts (drug pushers) that were ultimately responsible for millions of smoking-related deaths. If you smoke, please stop, it is suicide. Vaping is little better.

If the drug pusher/drug dealer is responsible for the community falling apart, for the spike in violent crimes, for carjackings and desperate home invasions, for tearing families apart, for mass imprisonment, for so much immense misery and also for the rise in taxes needed to be paid by the people for extra policing, extra security, imprisonment of drug abusers and for so much else, of course they need to be told, 'One strike and you're out!'

The reward from pushing killer drugs on children or on vulnerable categories of adults is immense because when you "need" your drug of choice, the drug pusher knows you will pay anything to obtain it, will pay any amount of gold to get just one more taste of it.

Yet, if the risk outweighs the reward, guess what happens. Nothing. No drug pushing. No drug dealing. Nothing happens.

Because the drug pusher desires rewards, happiness, 'stuff', and to enjoy himself. What they never desire is to be euthanized after earning their first $100 from selling fentanyl or cocaine to school children.

Once there is zero tolerance, once the nation and politicians and the judiciary all desire to raise up every community and stamp out apathy and masochism and crime and fear, once all are knowledgeable about the fact that drug dealing will result in them standing trial and facing capital punishment, it will be as though drug dealers commit suicide when insisting they continue being permitted to psychopathically and antisocially tear communities apart soul by soul when continuing to push drugs on people after knowing the consequence of their actions. Once capital punishment exists, the state does not kill the offender, no; the offender commits suicide by standing against the majority will. Hold a people's vote, hold a referendum on this subject; the majority desire it immediately everywhere.

Inform every citizen in the nation:

'Drug dealing will no longer be tolerated. Every drug dealer or drug mule or drug smuggler found guilty will face capital punishment.'

Instantly, communities and the nation will be wealthier and happier, and as less money needs to be spent on crime prevention and victim recovery and insurance claims and imprisonment and rehabilitation for criminals and recovery programmes for drug addicts, there will suddenly be huge resources available to assist those who felt the need to deal drugs and for those also who felt the need to consume drugs.

This fact will be publicised also, it must be, because the nation cares about all her children, including those temporarily lost, apathetic, pessimistic, cynical and in a rut. There should be no lost or forgotten people because if there are, they will tear communities apart, then towns and cities and then counties, then the entire state.

Achieving crime-free communities and a near 100% happy citizenry is not an easy task; yet it is achievable if the will and courage is there for this necessary fight. The needs of the many come first; the wants of the few must come last.

<u>Repeat Offenders</u>

Is some nations the 'three strike rule' exists, whereby a person needs to transgress thrice before being incarcerated for an extended period of time—not much of a punishment for him/her (as they are clearly unable to cope living a responsible and honest life outside of prison), it's more a punishment for taxpayers than anything else for being liberal and tolerant and giving second and third chances, a slap in the face for taxpayers in fact.

Imagine a man punches an eighty-year-old woman in her face because she does not give him her handbag as it contains her husband's ashes in an urn, which she takes everywhere with her because they were married for fifty-five years and she misses him desperately.

The old lady dies before the man's short trial can begin. Some think it was her broken heart that killed her (because the violent mugger refused to say there the bag and urn were when he was apprehended by the authorities); others think the injuries and the fall she sustained in the fight to keep her bag and husband with her caused her sudden ill health and death. Either way, the last man standing is he who punches eighty-year-old women in the face, in the dark, from behind.

Imagine that man, who manages to steal the handbag and the urn and the £25 in change in the bag after beating the woman, is simply given twelve months imprisonment and then released without any warning about what might happen to him should he repeat the same action or commit any other type of crime, especially violent crime against vulnerable and defenceless people.

However, if the violent bully is released and warned that, 'A second offence will be suicidal for you, you will literally be condemning yourself to instant euthanasia because capital punishment exists for repeat offenders,' will he even think about punching people in the face and stealing their property?

No, he will only think about legal routes to survival and happiness, beginning with contacting the authorities and local politicians as he searches for employment, as he searches for education and the tools needed to keep himself alive legally.

Do you want this man to receive only a two-year sentence for his second offence?

And if he is released again after serving the sentence you suggest he should serve (at huge cost to the taxpayer, as elderly folk count the pennies to be able to buy bread and pay for utilities) and goes on to yet again commit the same crime again, what then? Seven years in prison? Ten years? Fifteen years? And who is paying for this? Not him, not the clergy, not liberal elites and human rights advocates—you are paying for this, you, the average Joe, the manual labourer, the bus driver, the postman, the soldier, the police officer, the small business owner, the factory worker, the shop assistant, the cleaner, the builder, the farmer.

Gone would be my objections to overly lengthy sentences for violent criminals upon the occasion of Opt-In Taxation being ushered in and only certain folk (the minority) who desire to fund the prison system being required to pay extra taxation to keep those they wish to save from the rope alive as long as possible, as long as their finances will allow.

Yet, until such a time, the only sane recourse for situations such as this is euthanasia if the pattern of behaviour is certain, guaranteed in fact, to repeat itself again and again and again—not because of anything you have done wrong, not the fault of the system or the state, but oftentimes it is due to genetics, due to the offender and bully being a psychopath, literally having no empathy. One should never project themselves upon the defendant as it is rarely the case that the compassionate fellow looking from the outside in is in any way similar to he who physically beats pensioners in order to relieve them of their handbags. This is not bad judgement; this is bad blood. We must break this cycle, we must make a stand for law and order and justice.

Psychological Abusers/Antisocial Torturers

It is well known that music played at excessive volume is used to torture terror suspects in certain nations. It is very effective at destroying mental health very quickly; it is very effective at forcing enemies to comply with whatever it is that you wish them to comply with.

It has long been known that excessive noise is a weapon, as demonstrated by formations of men (armies) since ancient times banging shields, chanting, gutturally roaring and screaming and wailing and banging drums as they approached the gates of your city—loud noise and music dominates, depresses, confuses and intimidates; the lion's roar paralyses you.

Evidence of humankind knowing for the longest time that loud noises and music can be used to mentally harm people is found in an account of the most recent sack of Rome, which occurred in 1527, as mentioned elsewhere within this book, which describes noise torture being used at the same time (on the same day in fact) as extreme physical torture, with it being at that time deemed to be on a par with physical torture.

'Some were tortured by extreme thirst, <u>others by insupportable noise</u> and many were cruelly tortured by having their teeth brutally drawn. Others again were forced to eat their own ears, or nose, or their roasted testicles.'

—*Rome: The Biography of a City* by Christopher Hibbert.

Antisocial neighbour and noise pollution epidemics are widespread and growing due to a glaring loophole in the system in terms of stereo speakers and subwoofers being able to be weaponised and used for purposes of sadism and torture and extreme antisocial behaviour.

However, adding 'Psychological abusers/antisocial torturers' to the categories of those who should face capital punishment (only if their behaviour is continual and will never halt, even after complaints and attempts at re-education) is, of course, just a suggestion. It will be for the people and their representatives to decide what constitutes a serious crime and what does not. I merely offer suggestions and advice; the majority will decide what happens next. The book *Noise Pollution Kills*, a current work in progress, will explain in greater detail the devastating end results of antisocial neighbours and sadistic bullies utilising noise as a weapon against the majority in the 21st century.

What are we without our minds? We are nothing. The worst types of passive-aggressive, envious and cowardly psychological bullies in our midst of course understand this, especially when due to their condition or personality or choices they find themselves alone or in a small group of antisocial, anarchical and similarly nihilistic noise polluters, civilisation haters and neighbour haters.

Having one bad neighbour in a community of five hundred is enough to destroy the entire community as others will soon copy that person's behaviour. Others will begin causing stress and anxiety for the majority and soon loud music will be heard everywhere, even by those who are ill and recovering from strokes or bereavement, even by those who have worked a double shift and need a small amount of rest for the sake of their sanity.

The majority of the time, antisocial behaviour and noise pollution, or the weaponisation of music, is not "accidentally harmful", no; there is most often deliberate intent to cause harm. There is forethought; there is a desire to depress others, demotivate others and to bring everyone down.

The result is all too often folk moving away from the affected areas as crime rates soar and house prices sink and as life expectancy plummets due to antisocial neighbours and noise polluters reducing the lifespan of their neighbours by many years as a consequence of multiple factors, such as the incredibly detrimental end results of prolonged sleep deprivation and the harmful depression and anxiety and worsening physical health caused by exposure to constant bullying, domination, bombast and arrogance and intimidation. The majority of caring and thinking and sensitive citizens find themselves driven to drink more alcohol, smoke cigarettes or eat endless chocolate cakes as a means to find some sort of comfort in the hell they find themselves living within.

Domestic Abusers and Animal Abusers who emotionally, psychologically or physically sadistically bully and abuse innocents

That which is natural is good, yet that which is unnatural never is. It is natural to commit violence against the invader who seeks to enslave you and your family; yet it is unnatural to hurt your family violently or sexually or psychologically or all three, of course.

It is natural to fish or hunt in order to sustain yourself; yet it is unnatural to torture an animal or fish or any life form, for any reason. We do not observe this in the animal kingdom; great apes are vegan, yet they can and do kill animals who threaten them or trespass into their domains—but they do not sadistically, unnaturally hurt and torture and abuse these animals, they merely swiftly end their lives.

A truly heartless human knows that he can only kill his wife, husband, child or neighbour once, just once; but via threats and psychological torture and gaslighting and mental cruelty he can, in effect, kill them again and again and again, engendering mental illnesses, precipitating self-harm and depression and feelings of worthlessness.

Many are raised to believe that 'Sticks and stones can break my bones but words can never hurt me;' however, unfortunately this is not always the case. There are some who take everything to heart, who are deeply wounded by the cruel words of others, especially those they trust, who, either as a result of habitual intoxication or due merely to sociopathy or psychopathy or sadism continue to abuse them. These victims are transformed from happy souls into broken and self-hating shadows of their former selves. When the mind is broken, it matters not if the body is unbruised; a black eye merely proves the domestic abuser is unable to cow and bully their wife or child via cunning mind games and psychological bullying and gaslighting alone.

The rule of thumb should always be, 'Is this behaviour natural? Is this behaviour typical?' in the case of domestic abuse and in the case of cruelty to animals. These behaviours are neither natural nor typical and can never be condoned. Both the physical and mental health of all people as well as animals in our care is of fundamental importance.

Chapter Sixteen—The Confused Anti-Death Penalty Lobby

'I switched [from stabbing to strangling] because I was tired of getting blood on myself.'
—Gary Lee Sampson, who killed three people and attempted to kill a fourth. The psychiatrist on the case testified that Sampson did not suffer from any mitigating mental impairment.

You will have seen midnight candlelit vigils outside prisons in the USA and perhaps others nations also whenever wrongdoers and dangerous persons are to be executed in order to create justice, to serve as a deterrent and to protect all of the people, to make all of the people happy rather than just the fringe few standing outside with candles in their hands (0.1% of us).

However, these very same individuals, who are virtue signalling like crazy and signalling also that they are self-abnegating, masochistic victims-to-be who hate themselves and feel guilty for everything and thus deserve to be punished, would never desire the unrepentant killers, rapists and terrorists about to be executed to ever live with them in their houses with their children and other loved ones, would they? Would they?

No. Which is why they need to be silent.

Such irresponsible and emotionally out-of-control folk desire for 'someone else' to watch over these dangerous individuals who oftentimes (more often than not) are impossible to rehabilitate and will go on to reoffend again and again and again. The reoffending will continue for the remaining years of the criminal's life because there is an absolute lack of empathy within them. It has been proven that certain people derive pleasure from torturing and raping and killing innocents; they laugh at the relatives of their victims' loved ones in court.

I would strongly advise those who feel compelled to head towards the nearest prison whenever one of the worst of our number is scheduled to be euthanized to read two things, it will not at all take much time. The first is the story included in this book titled *Protect Me, You F***ing Fascist Scum!* and the second is the brief true story below:

Career criminal Carl Panzram was imprisoned on multiple occasions for first-degree murder, robbery and assault. After escaping a chain gang sentence in Texas, he abducted, assaulted and strangled a man then stole $35 from the victim. He later forced a railway detective/railway brakeman to rape a homeless man at gunpoint before throwing both of them off the train. For several months, he lured sailors onto his yacht, raped them and murdered them.

In Angola, he raped several children between the ages of eight and twelve and killed a boy of eleven, claiming later that, 'His brains were coming out of his ears when I left him and he will never be any deader.'

Back in the US he killed two small boys, beating one to death with a rock and strangling the other.

Eventually, Panzram received a twenty-five-years-to-life sentence.

When he arrived at Leavenworth Federal Penitentiary to begin serving his sentence, he is said to have warned the warden, "I'll kill the first man that bothers me."

Panzram was given a solitary job in the laundry room of the prison. On June 20, 1929, he beat the prison laundry foreman, Mr Robert Warnke, to death with an iron bar.

Panzram was sentenced to death for his latest in a long string of crimes.

He refused to allow any appeals of his sentence. He explicitly denied having any remorse for any of his crimes, stating, 'In my lifetime I have murdered twenty-one human beings, I have committed thousands of burglaries, robberies, larcenies, arsons and, last but not least, I have committed sodomy on more than 1,000 male human beings. For all these things I am not in the least bit sorry. I have no conscience so that does not worry me.'

In response to offers from death penalty abolitionists and from "human rights" activists who offered to advocate for him at the time, who tried to burden themselves and all taxpayers financially (preferring to pay to extend his life by many decades) whilst endangering the lives of every living American, Panzram made the following public statement:

"The only thanks you and your kind will ever get from me for your efforts on my behalf is that <u>I wish you all had one neck and that I had my hands on it</u>!"

Chapter Seventeen—Protect Me, You F***ing Fascist Scum!

'I am beyond good and evil. I will be avenged. Lucifer dwells in us all.'
—Richard Ramirez, who was convicted of thirteen murders, five attempted murders, eleven sexual assaults, and fourteen burglaries throughout California.

(This chapter originally appeared in the book *Wokeing Kills*)

Lucas Sanders had finally been caught, the serial killer and serial rapist having eluded the authorities for ten years as he destroyed the lives of thousands of people, whole communities being torn apart as a result of his sadism and barbarism. His victims numbered in the dozens, yet the harm caused affected untold amounts of lives.

When the unrepentant recidivist Sanders was finally recaptured (he was previously released after serving five years for multiple rapes), he spat at the police, spat at the judge and spat at the guards when confined in prison. He claimed his only regret was not raping and killing more people when he had the chance....

The jury produced a guilty verdict; the judge and all others present agreed as did Sanders, who waived his right to counsel and threatened to kill every man and woman present, continually, throughout the three-week trial.

He was sentenced to be executed. The execution was scheduled for one month later as the state and governor both agreed that it was inhumane to keep condemned prisoners alive for extended periods of time as they waited in limbo to be euthanized.

Everyone sane in the town wanted Sanders to hang.

Everyone sane in the county wanted him to hang.

His own family wanted him to hang.

The victims' surviving relatives, the wives and husbands, mothers and fathers, sons and daughters, sisters and aunties wanted Sanders to hang.

But guess who didn't? Self-righteous, bleeding-hearted woke neoliberals who believed that victims and their family members should pay higher taxes to keep bullies and killers and rapists alive indefinitely in prison, in relative luxury and comfort. Hardworking folk often fear where the money will come from to pay the electricity bill, many worrying if they will have enough cash to pay for groceries—are there such concerns in prison? Are there similar anxieties and fears?

No. It is a place of irresponsibility, retirement, drug abuse and idleness with the occasional bit of weightlifting—whose bright idea was that? What a great idea folks, let's make convicted unrepentant, violent, narcissistic bullies and sociopaths bigger and stronger, with their victims paying for the protein they consume and for the dumbbells they use to become even more of a threat upon release.

What a joke of a system, moronic—there is no real expectation that these folk will be genuinely rehabilitated or re-educated, which should be our first priority, yet not on their terms but on OURS.

***

Some folk hid behind their woke ideology, others hid behind their pacifist ideology whilst others hid behind selected, hand-picked sections from the New Testament in order to justify their presence outside the prison as the few dozen loud voices screamed and screamed like American Gretas for the release of the scumbag Sanders, who needed to be housed in a special cell on a special wing of the prison with extra cameras and security personnel in place to protect him, why?

Because among his victims were children, meaning most prisoners wanted to kill him immediately because, you see, when you are not a privileged woke liberal who wants for nothing, when you don't have a stake in life or property/land or wealth or connections or the nepotistic ability to get on (to advance, to become successful) even if you are very flawed (think Biden's son, the drug addict son who wrongly took all that money from Ukraine), the thing folk begin to cherish is people because it's the only thing they've got. The majority of folk in prison are good folk who have nothing, which is why they instinctively will lash out at any man who hurts a child.

The warden, who was inside the prison and heard the commotion outside, was frustrated and angered when the mob began banging on the gates of the prison and screaming as the commotion was disturbing the regular running of the facility, with visits for prisoners being cancelled due to many visitors complaining they received abuse from the "peace activists" and "lovers of humanity" outside as a result of them being misidentified as prison guards.

The vigil outside for the murderous Sanders became a 24/7 affair. Soon, all number of folk began arriving, from the last few remaining hippies to union representatives for some reason, to members of the clergy and a whole consortium of folk who clearly considered themselves to be superior and more knowledgeable and more empathic and more loving and more intelligent than everyone else including the jury and judge and the entire system as they DEMANDED Sanders not be killed.

The governor in that state, who happened to be the warden's brother, was also frustrated, both men relaying to the other that they were receiving thousands of cancel culture phone calls and emails and texts and social media posts from online "heroes" who were threatening to kill both men despite claiming to hate murder and death....

Before long, the vigils grew in size until it became a political issue and hot potato with more liberal TV networks and publications actively advocating for an end to capital punishment because killing bad guys upsets kind people who insist their chicken is boneless, skinless, featherless, bloodless and otherwise inoffensive so that their sensitivities are not offended.

As it seemed that all desired to save the mass murderer (because a TV news anchor's voice is seemingly worth ten million others in this barmy world of ours) the governor, who had the ultimate say as to whether or not there could be a pardon, did indeed use that power, but not because he had shamefully surrendered to groupthink, guilt-tripping, threats from extremists or was the latest in a long line of victims of cancel culture and political correctness, oh no, far from it. You see, the governor and his brother felt they'd had just about enough of irresponsible users and parasites who didn't live in the real world, who had too much power and privilege bossing them around when they were on the front lines, when they were responsible and hardworking and protective and stalwart.

Something snapped in the governor's mind. Maybe it was the rainbow flag cake sent to him in the mail that contained a bear trap; maybe it was the human faeces plastered over his home and car. It was something, something like that; one of those innumerable incidents caused the governor to shock absolutely everybody, and it occurred long before anyone expected....

It was only ten days into the big thirty-one-day countdown to the execution with many liberal news channels following the news story with a dramatic countdown clock, deliberately causing gentle folk, irresponsible and detached folk and very liberal and masochistic folk to become triggered and driven towards protest or indignation and at least, at the very least, into voting for the other party, the more liberal party who promised to get rid of drug control and borders and restrictions on everything—fun for all, well, for some.

The governor first told his brother the plan. He immediately agreed, knowing this would end vigils for monsters, certain that this single event, this grand spectacle would forevermore wake up the fools who caused themselves to be abused over and over and over again.

'Finally,' the governor told his brother, 'we'll be able to end violent crime, end rape and paedophilia, and undo the loud cult outside once and for all.'

***

The Press Conference

The governor rose to answer questions after reading his brief prepared speech, never looking at the cameras, never pausing to drink water or to smile or flirt with the public at home watching on—because the governor was focused on a very narrow goal, which he had to complete, which he certainly would complete, no longer a politician, no longer interested in the White House. Now all he thought of was restoring American confidence in the system, in the police, in the judiciary, in the criminal justice system and in the republic, the flag, all of it, America—the USA!

'Sam Friar, ABC. Governor, you can't be serious, can you? Are you are really pardoning him?'

'Ms Friar, most news networks have been in favour of the pardon and ending capital punishment. I am surprised your tone is one of shock, rather than glee and happiness.'

'But sir, we all … well—'

'You all expected this stubborn old fool to keep you guys and gals waitin' till the eleventh hour, right? Maybe the day before … and then, hey presto, I give you what you want, your ratings all go up, the woke liberals win and the taxpayer loses millions and millions 'cause Sanders will go on to outlive most current taxpayers in a comfortable, protected hotel room with free healthcare and free dental care, no bills for life and extreme comfort. No. No.'

'No?' the ABC reporter asked as the other journalists uncharacteristically sat in silence, not trying to butt in.

'*No,* I thought to myself, when all the bullying and attempts at cancelling me came rushing in and when all the same tactics were used against the warden.

'*No,* I thought. I will not do what you want me to do because the last thing you really want is for capital punishment to end. The last thing that you want is for me to pardon Sanders and the last thing that you want is for him to be released into your communities and rehoused there among your families because if this happened you wouldn't be able to shout, "Fascist! Fascist! Fascist!" and you would be forced to abandon your daydreaming and living in a dream world of bleeding-hearted liberalism because suddenly there would be an overabundance of human snakes in your communities, who we would leave there, who we would allow you to deal with, you alone to rehabilitate and "love better" as they swiftly began thinning the herd as your liberal complaints became lesser and weaker until we no longer heard a thing other than, "Governor, Warden, please bring a rope, these snakes are tormenting and killing us....'"

All reporters and journalists present were shocked yet guessed the man's angered outburst was the end product of all the death threats and attacks and threats of cancel culture and all the rest of it. So all believed his words to be false, that he merely sought to shake up the assembled audience; yet then he smiled as he shouted, 'Joe, turn on the big TV at the back; let these good folks enjoy the show.'

As the lights dimmed and a wall-mounted screen lit up behind him, showing a live feed of the outside of the facility in which the press conference was taking place, the governor, now joined by the warden (who was also smiling) declared, 'By popular request, I have pardoned Sanders and, further, I have released him into the custody and care of the pacifist, anti-death penalty vigil outside.'

Every arm shot up, everyone had a question; yet when the governor pointed to individual reporters, words failed to come out of their mouths as they watched the bizarre scene unfolding right before their eyes....

***

The stout gates of the prison slowly creaked open.

Sanders tentatively exited, continually looking over his shoulder at the shotgun-wielding guards, believing it a ruse, believing himself certain to be shot in the back at any second. Yet he wasn't. He exited fully before the gates swung shut, causing the ninety-seven-person-strong twenty-four-hour vigil community all to jump in shock at the terrific sound.

Sanders, however, did not jump as he was devoid of emotions in the traditional sense. He had no fear of anything, just a need to hurt, and his victims were always the weakest and most trusting and most naïve and the most tolerant and generous and loving and compassionate. Nice and kind people who trusted him always ended up raped and dead, every single time.

The vigil attendees began nervously applauding when they observed that their will was done, that the evildoer was pardoned, and not only pardoned but released into THEIR community.

Sanders licked his inglorious lips as he said, 'You are my saviours; that means you are now my keepers. I hope you've all got big families. I have a big appetite, you know....'

A few of the men in the vigil, who seemed like career protestors or professional protestors and complainers, stepped forward as if to put themselves between the female protestors and Sanders, instinct kicking in, yet were urged to step aside by their sisters and wives who insisted that Sanders was misunderstood, that he needed to be protected from fascists and from the system and from the patriarchy.

Sanders smiled as he reached the central point of the vigil of privileged liberals who were already in their minds planning on sacrificing their laundry room or their gymnasium at home in order to house the unrepentant killer, bully, rapist, paedophile and civilisation-hater Sanders.

The next thing he did was plunge a pen he'd been holding into the necks of three of the women nearest to him, killing two almost instantly and seriously injuring a third as everyone in the vigil surrendered to him. He took a fourth woman hostage as he literally growled at the onlookers and the millions watching on TV via the news conference as, by that time, every camera was trained upon the live images captured on the prison's external security cameras, audio included.

The governor knew that Sanders would reoffend, of course he did, but he had expected it to occur sometime later, he hadn't factored in Sanders immediately biting the hand that was trying to feed him; yet the lesson, he knew, would finally be learnt, he hoped.

Instinctively, the prison guards exited the prison, trained their weapons on Sanders and ordered him to release the woman, stop his murderous rampage and surrender to them.

Before Sanders could respond, the woman lying on the ground with blood squirting out of her neck, beginning to convulse, still holding the placard stating, 'FREE SANDERS!' summoned all her strength, defiance and rage to blurt at the guards, 'Don't arrest him, you fascist bullies. He had a bad childhood or might be a sociopath. He was born this way, who are you to judge? Don't shoot him, you f***ing fascist bas***ds!'

And as she shouted those illogical and confused words, her compatriot and fellow pacifist friend, who was being held tightly in Sanders' cruel grip as he began threatening to kill her also, meekly crowed to the guards in solidarity, 'Yeah ... and protect me, you f***ing fascist scum. Do your jobs, you plebs!'

***

Three Days Later

After the majority of journalists, reporters, politicians and celebrities all agreed that what the governor did was terrible, that his pardon of the killer (which many claimed to have wanted) was the real crime and what Sanders did was not a crime, was not his fault, Sanders was on cloud nine. TV networks began offering him millions for an interview; book deals were floated; Hollywood wanted to make a movie about his life. He knew that he was now basically God, able to kill at will without consequence, and every time he was released he'd able to kill and rape more people as a result of tolerance and liberalism and the masochistic and guilt-ridden, privileged few making the system suit themselves and their sensitivities.

The governor had been told that he would soon have to retire, the powers that be in his party, the donors and folk in the business world all needed him to leave sooner rather than later as he was bad for the brand; in truth, they were cowed by the cancel culture fascist bullies who wished to be the only voice heard.

He'd hinted to a few reporters and colleagues that he would be leaving soon, so the anger and blame first shifted off Sanders to the governor then off the governor and onto anyone and everyone who was pro capital punishment as, once again, the liberal reaction to Sanders' killing spree (as he knew would be the case) was liberals and Christians and the woke few demanding an end to the death penalty.

It was like a macabre, depressing groundhog day. This is why Sanders killed those women—because he knew that less than five minutes later, their loved ones would be advocating for him and breaking down the prison gates in order to, in a Stockholm syndrome and self-hating and self-sabotaging fashion, liberate the devil.

As the attention was off him momentarily, the governor spent some time on social media, where he anonymously encouraged more pacifists and advocates for higher taxation and neoliberal woke groups and individuals all to descend upon the prison in order to demand that Sanders was not charged with the new murders and the attempted murder and the hostage taking—and they did. They took his bait.…

✳✳✳

The moment the governor counted 1000 woke, pacifist, privileged East/West Coast supremacist, groupthink, vanity-tech-owning neoliberals (that's WPPEWCSGVTONL for those obsessed with labels, acronyms and creating modern apartheid) outside the prison, he gave the order once again. 'Let him out, he's pardoned; open the gates!'

For the second time, Sanders was thrown to the mob begging for him to be pardoned. They got their Barabbas.

This time, however, half of the vigil ran away, not wishing to die; yet the other half remained, merely hoping that they would be spared.

And they were this time because the warden had spoken with Sanders an hour prior, telling him that what he did in the comfort of his own home was his own business, as in, if he and his saviours wanted to kill one another in their places of middle-class or elite privilege, then they could go ahead, but no more killing outside the prison. Sanders guessed the warden would kill him (shotguns, remember) if he once again killed in public, so this time his approach was different.

Walking through the crowd of those who did not flee, he found Jolene, a retired school teacher from a small town and widow of the local preacher, who supported over twenty charities despite not being all that wealthy, not after the accident that left her confined to a wheelchair that is, that left her alone with her cat now that her husband had passed. Sanders read all these things on her face at once, of course, because he was a cunning and deceptive Machiavellian sheep in wolf's clothing. *Yes,* he thought, *I will start with this one then work through this woke group like a hot knife through butter. Is this my birthday or something? Hallelujah! This is heaven for me, heaven!*

***

Jolene and her neighbours and her beloved cat were found in her burnt-out house. It was Sanders who phoned the police. He had become bored, he missed the attention and the cameras and the notoriety, which is likely why he visited many of his supporters who had visited him in prison, who had written to him and thus given him their addresses. He viciously executed them one by one, which he found particularly humorous due to them trying so hard to prevent him being executed. The joke was lost on them. He callously consumed popcorn as they begged in vain for mercy.

Now he was back in prison again, guess who was in hot water? Yes, the governor, rather than the rapist-killer, with all the blame and rage and anger being shifted onto him as though he, not Sanders, was the sadist and bully and criminal and wrongdoer.

As a result of once again being the whipping boy for irresponsible cowards who wrongly believed that taxes would fix every problem and it was always someone else's responsibility to protect them and to keep serial killers alive for decades and decades and decades for some bizarre reason, the governor decided to create a social media post in which he said only, 'Who would like me to call a press conference for today in regards to pardons?'

Suddenly, amazingly, all the complaints and shouts of 'Fascist!' and the threats to cancel the governor, to cancel the system, to defund the police, to defund everything and everyone whilst increasing taxes to pay for the astronomical costs of prisons and housing unrepentant monsters ended, ended dead, just as the few remaining fools at the vigil departed immediately upon hearing the news of another press conference being threatened.

Suddenly, the desire for tolerance of criminals and high taxes for victims was no longer in vogue, just as releasing bad guys was no longer in vogue, because suddenly folk had woken up, really woken up, and they would never go back to sleep because they never wanted crime, apathy, weakness or suicidal wokeness to return.

Chapter Eighteen—Woke Democratic Hypocrisy

'I live for the hunt—my life.'
—David Berkowitz, who killed six young people and wounded others. The killing spree terrorised many New Yorkers and achieved worldwide notoriety.

Woke liberals who are vehemently opposed to the death penalty are also, interestingly, vehemently opposed to holding any type of nationwide people's referendum on <u>any subject</u> as they desire minority rule, liberal elite minority rule.

These people hate democracy, despise people power and would cry and scream to prevent referendums on immigration, welfare, voluntary taxation, socialised medicine, capital punishment and much else.

The same very well-educated woke liberals (who are mostly supremacists and fascists in denial, who eternally desire the class system to remain in exactly the same way, forever unchanged) whilst hating real democracy and hating majority rule also never desire to live with or alongside the people they heroically save from the gallows.

They wish for such people to live somewhere else, in another town or country, somewhere else far, far away from them and their precious family. In this way they are no different from those who demand open borders yet who live in areas where no immigrants could ever afford to purchase land, apartments or houses.

If you live in Martha's Vineyard or Mayfair and have an 'Open the Borders Now, We Have Room!' poster in your window, it is irrelevant as Martha's Vineyard and Mayfair are different worlds, different universes in comparison to Harlem, Brixton or a trailer park.

What woke, liberal, privileged rich elites are truly saying when they claim to be pro-open-borders is, 'Please move to a part of the USA/UK where you will find no woke folk, no liberal elites and no leftist thought leaders. Come here and lower wages for our native poor whilst pushing up rents.'

When you prevent an execution, you are not saving a life so much as you are endangering hundreds of other lives, including potentially your own in a bizarre act of masochistic self-sabotaging stupidity.

Am I wrong? Will woke liberals house rapists and murderers and paedophiles alongside their children following early release from prison?

No. I am not wrong; they are, and when regular folk become fed up with criminals being rehoused in their neighbourhoods, in non-woke neighbourhoods, the woke tune will very quickly change as no one, even the most ideologically and partisan blinded and blinkered bleeding-hearted liberal, high and intoxicated and ever distracted by their own virtuousness, would ask a convicted paedophile to babysit their children for them, but these same folk are happy for paedophiles to walk among us, to prey on our young ones, to be protected, nurtured, loved and doted on and fed and watered and given free healthcare, housing and new identities after destroying many lives.

Those who save wrongdoers from the gallows should be the ones who become eternally responsible for the wrongdoers.

If the state is not permitted to protect the people, then the "saviours" who prevented the state from euthanizing clear and present dangers to the safety of us all must be forced to bear the full tax bill and full care bill for housing and keeping alive paedophiles, rapists, drug pushers and terrorists for the remainder of their days.

And when this long overdue change occurs, when victims no longer have to pay taxes to keep alive the worst criminals who should no longer draw breath, I wonder how many folk will continue to identify as being woke on social media.

Perhaps a handful, maybe half a dozen only, as all others will know that to declare yourself woke in a truly responsible era is to invite every refugee, murderer, terrorist and paedophile into your home; otherwise, you will be deemed merely a virtue-signalling hypocrite, supremacist and liar.

Chapter Nineteen—In the News

'Not too long, I had other things to do.'
—Ed Gein, after he was asked just how long he wore the skin masks he created from his victims. The 'Mad Butcher of Plainfield' confessed to killing two women. When authorities searched Gein's home, they found horrifying, handmade trophies and keepsakes from the bones and skin of the bodies.

What is the difference between Britain today and the Britain of, say, sixty years ago?

The main difference, I contest, is the removal of the death penalty, which acted as a deterrent for a whole host of crimes, including rape and paedophilia.

Do searches yourself to confirm what I will say next is accurate (please fact check all of my many books). I have only used a few news reports; there are many more that confirm my assertion that the removal of the death penalty (capital punishment) has massively fuelled murder, paedophilia, rape, and, more recently, terrorism.

Here are several recent articles from the BBC, which, bear in mind, is owned and operated by the UK state/crown, who are both opposed to the reintroduction of the death penalty.

These articles were not published in an attempt to help this book; rather, they were published to highlight the failings of law enforcement, the probation service and the judiciary.

None of these or any other BBC articles or mainstream media articles is advocating for a return of the rope as a remedy for millions of violent rapes that have occurred in the UK following the abolition of capital punishment, with many believing the reported figures to be on the low side; the real figure is likely frighteningly higher.

'Sex crimes reported in Scotland at 50-year high.'

'Sex offences recorded in Scotland have risen to a 50-year high despite a drop in overall crime figures.'

'The statistics showed a drop in reported crime in 2021-22, to its lowest level since the early 1970s.'

'According to the data, cases of rape and attempted rape rose by 9% to 2,498 last year - accounting for almost one in five (17%) of all reported sexual crimes.'

'Scottish Conservative justice spokesman Jamie Greene said: "These grim statistics confirm that violent and sexual crime is spiralling out of

control.""'
—28 June 2022, BBC online news

'Police in England and Wales have recorded the highest number of rapes and sexual offences in 20 years.'

'Forces recorded 194,683 sexual offences in 2021-22, including 70,330 rapes, the highest number since records began in 2002/03.'

'The number of sex offences recorded by forces in England and Wales has more than doubled in the past seven years, from 88,576 in 2014/15 to 194,683 in 2021-22.'

'Rape offences have nearly doubled in the past six years, from 36,320 in 2015-16 to 70,330 in the year to March.'

'Rape offences at highest recorded level.'
—21 July 2022, BBC news

This is the price of tolerance. This is what happens when you care more about convicted rapists and paedophiles and antisocial and inhuman elements than you do about innocents. How long will we sacrifice our children and sisters and mothers in this way? How long will we remain weak and at the mercy of snakes and wolves? When will sanity and strength and courage be restored?

It is the same story everywhere, from the USA in states where the death penalty is no more to European nations, to Africa and Asia, with the common theme always being a massive surge in violent and sexual offences and murder and terrorism after the judiciary and police have become liberalised and made progressive, effectively tying the hands of our protectors. It makes us all lambs to the slaughter, afraid to defend ourselves lest we be sent to prison for killing a rapist or mugger or home invader or terrorist.

If you desire to keep seeing sickening headlines like the ones above, do nothing other than burn this book and you will guarantee your family and community will continue being raped and abused.

Yet if you desire to read only positive, uplifting and optimistic headlines as crime becomes a thing of the past, as order and sanity are restored, give a copy of this book to a friend or neighbour (make copies of it, get the message out, you have my full consent to do so) and demand a referendum on capital punishment, demand to no longer be forced to pay ever higher taxes to fund the lifestyles of killers, paedophiles, rapists and corrupt politicians and the wolves in sheep's clothing hiding among the clergy.

If you do nothing, you are complicit.

If you do something, you are part of the solution.

I cannot do this alone, you cannot do this alone, but together we can move mountains; together we can end crime and fear and disorder and violence and rape. Together we can win; together we will strangle apathy and surrender and weakness and together we will then enjoy the beautiful calm and peace and reborn civilisation founded on responsibility, self-control, self-governance, duty, righteousness and unbridled love for all peaceful humans everywhere and zero tolerance for crime or criminals of any stripe.

There are no excuses, there is no mitigation. We have suffered enough; you have suffered enough, no more. Demand better. Demand that your family is protected.

Chapter Twenty—The 'Real Jesus' and Why the Clergy Only Temporarily Hate Capital Punishment

'I want the world to know I killed these men, as cold as ice. I've hated humans for a long time. I killed them in cold blood, real nasty.'
—Aileen Wuornos

He who seeks to interrupt a legal execution when the vast majority desire it is either responsible for many previous crimes and thus wishes to make the nation a more liberal and tolerant and forgiving place for reasons of self service and their own life being extended (they fear judgement for their own wrongdoings or transgressions) or merely it is due to them being so sensitive and so full of disgust for blood and death and the ending of a human life because it reminds them they are mortal and vulnerable and that they will surely die one day and this reality vexes them, this realisation troubles their psyche.

In the UK, for hundreds of years there existed capital punishment, until the 1960s, when it suddenly ended, with the clergy and feminists and atheist neoliberals (an odd alliance) leading the charge to ban executions for any reason.

Interestingly, this was the period in time when the common folk, aided by unions and newfound freedoms and interconnectivity and sharing of information via multiple means, were starting to speak up for themselves. Complaints about living conditions increased, rights were demanded, complaints about teachers and politicians and the clergy physically or sexually abusing them began to abound.

It was around this time that multiculturalism began and with it, in places such as the UK, white Christian flight and demographic change, which directly led to the erosion of congregations and a rejection of the clergy by many people who had previously relied on this group/class for much and thus always trusted them and remained faithful, even when their children reported that they were being routinely sexually assaulted by priests and cardinals.

The clergy were happy for stones to be cast when they had all the power and mass was delivered in Latin to folk who could not read or write; yet, when the poorest were suddenly well educated, had access to information and transport and interconnectivity and were represented by non-clergy groups such as unions and fringe (far right/far left) parties and political movements, suddenly the clergy in places such as the UK insisted that we should 'liberalise the judiciary' immediately and stop killing paedophiles and serial killers and unrepentant, psychopathic monsters intent on destroying even more lives.

It is coincidental timing, is it not, that as congregations dwindled and folk began thinking for themselves and becoming more empowered, the clergy demanded an end to the death penalty for crimes against children.

Not only were the clergy historically very pro-capital punishment, they consented to the Christian-on-Christian violence and inhuman bloodshed that occurred in both WWI and WWII without a single priest or bishop or cardinal ever daring to even attempt to walk between the two groups of Christians slaughtering one another. There was no attempt to make peace, no martyrs for peace, not at all.

The clergy also supported and encouraged the Crusades, the Spanish Inquisition, witch hunts, the near extinction of cats throughout Europe, the transatlantic slave trade (the first ship bringing slaves to the New World being named The *Good Ship Jesus*) and many other inhuman, violent and murderous acts down through the centuries—with an insane amount of innocent blood on the hands of various branches of the clergy, an insane and hard to fathom amount in fact.

However, fast-forward to the 1960s in the UK and, all of a sudden, now that the native poor were no longer brow-beaten, cowed or under the thumb of the clergy and monarch as social liberation and liberalism spread, the clergy demanded an instant end to capital punishment. Their tune changed for self-serving reasons of course, with this sudden change of heart not born out of love or compassion but out of pragmatism and self-service as they sought to protect the rapists and murderers within the clergy ... from the people, from judgement.

When the clergy fears being caught out, they lurch towards liberalism, as in the case of 'he who casts the first stone'. Yet, when the clergy feels above the law and the 'gatekeepers of heaven' they are very much authoritarian, draconian and desire each and every criminal to be immediately executed (so long as he is not a member of the clergy of course) to reassure the people, to create good order and to distract attention away from the crimes committed by certain members of the clergy who are corrupted by power or who were psychopathic paedophiles long before joining the clergy.

An interesting means to reinstating capital punishment in places such as the UK would be almost everyone returning to the Church, absolutely packing them out—standing room only.

Imagine if suddenly almost every man and woman, boy and girl threw their TVs and radios and smartphones and internet modems into the Mariana Trench (which would only help, which couldn't hurt anyone incidentally) and chose instead to only listen to the clergy, every single word and bit of advice they had to give. Imagine also that many of the self-segregating, non-Christian migrant groups also abandoned their tribal religions in favour of the native religion (when in Rome and all that) and also decided to go to church every single Sunday and give huge amounts of donations to the church and clergy.

What would happen next, after a complete reversal of fortunes for the clergy, after now becoming rich and powerful and being the only source of information and guidance, with the media now being fully ignored, with the entire population basically servants to the clergy, owned body, mind and soul, as it was for hundreds upon hundreds of years of strict orthodoxy? Capital punishment would return!

Yes, within a very brief period of time, the throngs of good people who overfilled every church in the land would begin begging priests and bishops and cardinals and popes and archbishops to save not only their souls but also their lives and sanity by robustly dealing with sociopaths, sadists, psychopaths and nihilistic addicts who were, as they always have been, destroying civilisation one piece at a time, one victim at a time.

The clergy, seeing the people suffering inside the church as a result of donations, seeing them suffer as a result of corruption and abuse of parishioners' children within the new replenished clergy, as a result of new flocks of men flooding in and also as a result of the crime and evil committed by the few outside the church, would need to very hurriedly make a pragmatic choice:

1.   End all suffering for the flock: No more financial tithes, no more paedophilia, no more clergy corruption and no more rape/murder/home invasions as a result of the deterrent of capital punishment—violent crime in the UK is currently at the highest record level since the abolition of the death penalty in the 1960s. Just a coincidence, right?

2.   End corruption/crimes against children in the Church.

3.   End tithes/donations to the clergy—necessitating getting a real, regular day job and being forced to volunteer to be a priest/vicar/pastor.

4.   Or ignore the suffering caused by tithes and donations, ignore the abuses of the clergy, ignore clergy corruption and instead throw their full weight and support behind bringing back capital punishment after they were intrinsic in ending it just a few decades earlier.

In every conceivable scenario the clergy chooses option 4.

If the clergy, when again having total control and domination did nothing, allowed crime to continue to soar, allowed the people to become poor whilst being terrified of violent criminals in tandem with being laid low by tithing and being occasionally (or systemically even) abused by certain members of the clergy, they would know for a certainty that history would repeat itself. Folk would eventually stop visiting church on Sunday, would stop throwing their finite resources into the collection plate and thus the clergy would be defunded and forced to find new employment and purpose elsewhere.

It is only because people became smart and empowered that the clergy ended capital punishment.

If the people agree to again become dumb puppets who never complain and who give everything, including their lives even when the clergy and state demand they do in order to kill other Christians elsewhere, capital punishment shall instantly return, instantly.

Would Jesus have taught the 'do not cast the first stone' lesson to folk if they were all believers in him and sat in his church every week listening to his every word, following his every order and self-abnegating as requested by him as they tithed and tithed and impoverished themselves as instructed to do so? No, the answer is no.

Picture the scene. Imagine two weeks before Jesus first told folk not to cast stones thousands had built a church and called it the Church of Christ after witnessing his miracles.

They constructed pews and waited excitedly and expectantly for Jesus to arrive, to see the good works they had done, where he would of course be expected to lead and shepherd and protect them, rather than guilt-tripping them or shaming them into becoming liberal or tolerant or "open minded".

Jesus walks into the church, his church, built for him by his people, those who witnessed his miracles—the only reason people follow Jesus as his philosophy alone (birthed in a time when there was no congregation, which mirrors the 1960s in the UK as congregations dwindled) does not put bums on seats. No miracles = no Christianity.

Jesus brings with him a simple wooden collection plate that he has whittled himself; after all, he is a carpenter.

The folk inside, already poor and downtrodden, place a few shekels or whatever they have into the collection plate as he begins delivering a sermon.

The next week, the same thing happens as Jesus ponders introducing the 'do not cast the first stone' line of thinking.

The next week, Jesus comes again to the church, with the 'do not cast the first stone' (anti-capital punishment liberal doctrine) sermon now fully fleshed out in his mind as he plans to tell his huge audience that they should forgive bullies, rapists, paedophiles, killers and all else … but then he sees something that troubles him terribly.

As his congregation, whom he instructs not to throw the oppressor and invader (the Roman) off their backs and fight for freedom and salvation and self-respect and human dignity, are busy emptying their meagre pockets of their meagre resources whilst silently sobbing. Jesus notices that 70% of his congregation have black eyes, split lips, broken fingers, smashed eye sockets, broken orbital bones and many missing teeth as well as many arms in slings.

Is this because I told them last week to 'turn the other cheek' I wonder, Jesus thinks.

'Who did these things to you, my loyal faithful flock who built this mighty church, this testament to your belief in me and in your faith in me to be your protector and shepherd and friend and ally in life and in death? Tell me now, right this instant, who did these terrible things to you? How came you to be so beaten and hurt and laid low?'

They reply, 'It's okay, Jesus, we can take it. We are all sinners, after all, so who are we to complain? You taught us that. We will keep giving to the church and believing more as we get hurt more by the bullies and psychopaths and sadists and unempathic psychopaths in our midst, this is our cross to bear.'

'No!' Jesus would have surely said, if he loved his people and desired to maintain his congregation for any length of time. 'I am your shepherd and you are my flock. I will guard you one and all in both life and in death for I am not your boss but your leader, not a detached parasite but one of your number, of humble roots, of the people, of you. I am you as you are me; this cannot stand, this violence, this sadism, this torment. This bullying of my flock must end immediately!'

'But how, Jesus? How can we fight back when you tell us it is wrong to fight back, wrong to kill, wrong to punish wrongdoers because everyone is guilty meaning no one can be punished?'

'The law. The law of man. Justice. Judges. The will of the good and of the righteous majority will end this cruel barbarism and suffering. If the law and judges and the state working with the clergy cannot end your torment and suffering, you will continue visiting my church every single week with new bruises all about your faces and bodies as well as the invisible bruises in your heart caused by deep fear and anxiety, misery and powerlessness. This cannot stand, I refuse to see my flock being abused continually and laid low and depressed. You should wear no bruises on your faces, no bruises in your hearts, you should be strong and proud; your heads should be held up high for you are no worse than those who beat you. You are better, infinitely better, and your lives and happiness matter infinitely more than the lives of those who bully and rape and rob and kill.'

Jesus, thinking about his next course of action, remembered the 'do not cast the first stone' sermon that he had planned to introduce that very day to his flock, his bruised and battered and debased and impoverished flock; yet after witnessing them at such a low ebb whilst being so wholeheartedly enthusiastic and faithful and all believing and absolutely desperate for salvation, he put that sermon out of his mind, thinking to himself, *That's the last thing the flock needs. Maybe if they hadn't built the church, maybe if they ignored me I would have introduced that sermon; yet, now they have come to me and rely on me to lead them, how can I disarm them? How can I feed them to the wolves? How can I betray them by whipping them with guilt as I equate their little wrongdoings, their little transgressions to rape and murder and sadistic bullying and torture? I cannot, I will not, because that sermon would enable wrongdoing, endanger my flock, and ensure that those bruises would remain in place forever, in this world and the next.*

Chapter Twenty-One—More Taxes That Should Go … and Why

'I like children, they are tasty.'
—Albert Fish, a child rapist and cannibal. His most well-known crime is the murder of Grace Budd, a small girl from New York City whom he kidnapped, dismembered, and ate.

There is definitely a case for removing additional tax burdens from the poor, especially native poor; born and bred poor need to come first, irrespective of location—should the Martian native poor come first or should human poor who arrived there with begging bowls come first?

Employment taxes being removed, or massively diminished, would be step one.

Beyond this obvious tax, there will be many stealth taxes because those who govern and who also have cocaine habits are in equal measure crafty and greedy.

The additional or stealth taxes include property tax, inheritance tax, death taxes, and car taxes.

If your political representatives and the liberal elites who guide woke, progressive high-tax policies are absolutely ruining your community, finances, culture, harmony, sanity and nation as a whole, if they are destroying your mental health and peace, if you do not feel safe after their changes, if you feel suicidally depressed and driven to fentanyl or fast food or whiskey for emergency escapism, why should you be paying a single cent in tax to those responsible for your mental, physical and financial decline?

It would be madness to volunteer cash to the ideologues, sell-outs and fat cats in ivory towers when there is a choice to allow wealthy socialistic liberals who claim to care about all people and love all people to solely bear the financial burden—because they are the only ones who desire these policies.

The unending insults about 'rednecks' and 'white trash' from "enlightened" coastal liberal elite communities may have been a big own goal. All that bullying and poor-bashing designed to mask liberal elites' fear and weakness and inability to lead and unworthiness to lead was, in actual fact, little more than the privileged woke liberals shooting themselves in the foot as those same long-bullied and persecuted and dehumanised members of the community will of course not volunteer to fund the system that hates them a moment longer. Once the people can choose to volunteer taxes or withhold them, it is game over for the elite bullies in sheep's clothing.

The final tax to go would be VAT. Value added tax, or sales tax—which applies to the purchase of food and services and goods, etc.

Imagine that crime has massively increased due to short-sighted liberal policies designed to make folk happy, which ended up making everyone drug addicts and homeless and mentally ill and violent. Why would you continue to tolerate paying high prices for goods because the government has added a huge amount of tax atop the purchase? If you are being treated like trash, you want to pay trash prices, not liberal elite prices that only they can afford.

If you want more abortions and more immigration; if you want to house terrorists, murderers, paedophiles and traitors in prison rather than the graveyard; if you want to fund the lifestyles of criminals and non-contributing members of society in perpetuity, you and you alone should be paying for these things. <u>You and you alone</u>.

This is an opportunity for the most virtuous wealthy, privileged, liberal elites and benevolent corporations and tech companies and Silicon Valley to step up, to demand this referendum, this people's vote, and insist they volunteer to pay so much more in taxes in order to get everything they want in life because they want to make terrorists and rapists and murderers and corrupt politicians and traitors happy and comfortable.

So they should be allowed to, but by God they should not compel you to join in with their high-taxation lunacy, which is crippling nation after nation. We are sinking, we are in debt; we need voluntary taxation immediately to create balance and true democracy.

In addition, voluntary taxation is the guarantor that civil wars will be prevented due to both left and right getting everything they desire. Voluntary taxation makes this possible, yet we may find that the leftist enthusiasm for high taxes will wane then disappear if only progressive, liberal wokeists are paying taxes for certain projects and departments.

At that stage, we will have the opportunity to refind ourselves and refind common sense, stoicism and resilience. We need this change deeply if we wish to endure as a species.

Chapter Twenty-Two—How to Democratically Silence Fake Saviours and Virtue Signallers Opposed to Capital Punishment

'You think of people as things... As much as I say I wanted to stop, there probably would've been others.'

—Joel Rifkin, who killed as many as seventeen women. He dismembered the body of Heidi Balch, removing her teeth and fingertips and putting her head in a paint can. Rifkin casually opened up about his crimes and compared quitting his murder addiction to quitting smoking.

If you prevent a serial killer, a terrorist, corrupt politician or a paedophile from being legally euthanized, virtue is not bestowed upon you. No one will applaud you; you are not considered wise, benevolent or righteous; rather, you are (and will be thought of as) a foolish, detached, irresponsible and elite masochist who refuses to grow up and who is happy to impoverish the people via them being forced to pay higher taxes whilst being willing to gamble with their lives and the lives of their children because your own feelings, sensitivities, wants and "principles" are more important to you than the safety of the people and the nation.

You keep what you save; you are responsible for what you save, meaning if you spare the life of the worst, most unrepentant and dangerous and violent criminals, they are now solely *your* responsibility, in terms of finances and housing, healthcare and welfare.

Gone be the madness of forcing 100% of people to pay to house, feed and protect those whom the majority desire to be legally executed or at a minimum exiled and stripped of all property, assets, citizenship and rights following a lengthy prison sentence funded by the human rights activists and the clergy and similar groups of self-hating, self-abnegating, out-of-touch, privileged masochists.

If folk truly desire to "save" those whom the rest of us desire to be legally euthanized, *they* and *they* alone should bear the entire burden of caring for these people for the remainder of their natural lives. Only *their* purse should be hurt; only *their* homes should be used to house these people; only *they* should be expected to pay for their healthcare and dental work and all else they require.

Before long, the native voices against capital punishment will quieten after realising they only want to save serial killers and paedophiles and terrorists when everyone is footing the huge bill for their massive taxpayer-funded life extensions.

Virtue and principles shall fly out of the window when the gaggle of unempathic monsters arrives at the door of human rights activists and opponents of capital punishment needing a roof over their head, needing food and alcohol, cigarettes and gold and all else they desire, which many of them have previously killed to obtain.

Immediately, in a nanosecond, gone will be the preaching when human rights activists are confronted with the reality of being compelled to 'put their money where their mouth is' by living their faith and principles, by personally taking a risk, by personally sharing the fruits of their labours with those they were so desperate to save … but then there are folk abroad who may make a complaint or two about the citizenry refusing to be victims any longer by insisting capital punishment be the tool to emancipate them mind, body and soul.

<u>International Relations</u>

If foreign nations have an objection to the majority will being done in your nation, do not become angry. There is no need for bad diplomacy or rifts, no; rather, this creates a great opportunity for compromise.

An example of how one could manoeuvre out of a situation whereby other nations are reacting in scornful or judgemental or critical manner about capital punishment being reintroduced is 'transfer of citizenship post-imprisonment'.

Example:
Germany introduces capital punishment for a number of serious crimes.
France complains publically about Germany legally euthanizing paedophiles, serial killers and terrorists.
Germany responds:
'If France wishes to extend the life of all German paedophiles and German terrorists we invite France to pay to fund their prison stay for a period of twenty years, and thereafter, once the prison term is completed in Germany, the offenders will be deported to France, where they will instantly become French citizens and thus the responsibility of every French taxpayer and citizen. If France does not agree to these terms, France should not tell Germany what to do, just as Germany does not tell France what to do.'

Who thinks France or any other nation will ever again interfere in the sovereign justice system of Germany, which exists to service all of her law-abiding citizens?

If clergies, NGOs or entire nations are critical of you refusing to extend the life of clear and present dangers to the most vulnerable people in your nations, invite the NGO, clergy or foreign nation to pay for the imprisonment of your worst offenders and then invite them to adopt the same folk following the completion of the prison sentence, all of them, absolutely all of them.

If a very liberal nation did indeed, foolishly, choose to import thousands of killers and paedophiles and known terrorists from around the world, it would not take long for the citizens of that land to change how they think and how they vote.

What would likely, ironically, occur as a result of pacifists and human rights activists and paedophile savers and terrorist savers compelling their nation to import and grant citizenship to tens of thousands of killers and traitors and corrupt politicians and baby killers would be those same pacifists and human rights activists needing to apply for sanctuary and refuge in another nation before too long as their normal, regular and healthy-minded countrymen and women would come to consider them fifth-columnists, crime enablers and dangerous masochists who desire suffering to be shared collectively.

Most French folk would refuse to pay higher taxes to house another nation's killers and rapists and terrorists. Protests would begin immediately; folk would demand all NGOs leave their nation; folk will demand the government resign immediately. It would be a huge scandal, especially during a time of recession and migrant crises and crime waves and pandemics and wars in the Middle East and in Eastern Europe (as there are currently); this would be one liberal step too far, far too far.

If other countries do not accept the condemned criminals, they should be silent and if their taxpayers do not wish to pay huge sums of money to house, rehabilitate, police and feed and water and provide free healthcare and new identities to thousands of unrepentant paedophiles and terrorists, why should any group of taxpayers within a democratic framework in any land be expected to shut up, open their purses, shut their mouths, and fund the huge life extensions of the very worst and most dangerous reoffending, unrepentant bullies, civilisation haters and wrongdoers?

If a state rejects them, why must all the people accept them? And if no liberals and no priests want terrorists, serial killers or rapists rehomed with them and their family, why should the people tolerate the literal scum of the earth being deposited into their communities, which were made safer when the criminal was placed in prison but are again now in jeopardy and sent into panic mode when the bully, rapist or killer or terrorist is released to offend and offend and offend again?

Chapter Twenty-Three—Mental Illness and Excuses

'I intended to kill them all.'
—Lee Boyd Malvo who, along with an accomplice, killed ten people. When Malvo heard that all their victims had not died, he responded that he wished they had.

Not every sociopath, psychopath, schizophrenic or person born with learning disabilities, who suffers from bipolar disorder or PTSD, or who is classified as low-functioning kills or rapes. Having a mental illness, being atypical, being born differently, having a disability is no excuse, is no defence whatsoever when you have transgressed against the people and the community. A threat is a threat; a criminal is a criminal.

The irony of the liberal argument that 'He cannot be sentenced to capital punishment because he has a mental illness' is that throughout all of recorded history, it has never been the case that the mentally healthy have been legally euthanized—as those who are 'in their right mind' tend not to rape, kidnap, kill and commit acts of terrorism.

'It is not their fault' brings no solace to victims, does not reassure the community and ensures the offender will continue offending and reoffending for the remainder of their lives.

In the West, we love dogs. When there is a house fire, I, like most Westerners, will be very concerned about saving humans from the burning building yet equally concerned about ensuring all animal life is saved also, including dogs.

However, if a dog is mentally ill, if a dog kills its owner and afterwards mauls a baby and it is deemed certain that the same dog will kill and keep killing until being euthanized, everyone in the community who loves dogs, who would run into a burning building in order to save the life of a dog, would suddenly, collectively, desire for the dangerous, mentally ill dog to be painlessly and expediently euthanized. No moronic death row waiting period, no last meals, no misplaced sentimentality but a swift resolution, one that guarantees the animal's suffering immediately ends just as the threat to the community immediately ends also.

Humans are little different.

A serial killer will of course be deemed to be mentally ill, just as a man who rapes and kills ten babies will similarly be deemed mentally ill. Should the mental illness afford these people protection? Should it be a mitigating factor? No, of course not.

Sane people who are intelligent and law-abiding and mentally healthy do not rape, rob or kill, meaning almost every single instance of capital punishment will involve a mentally healthy victim (rape victim, murder victim, paedophilia victim) and a mentally ill offender.

The defence of those with mental illnesses who rape, rob, abuse and kill those without mental illnesses is a sort of Marxist-Jesuit approach to justice and law and order, as in the rich man and poor man, as in the man with poor mental health deserves a 'leg up' due to not having the advantage of having good mental health/good genes. However, oftentimes, the offender and the victim both have mental illnesses; yet, even in such cases, folk ignore the fact that the victim was as mentally ill, as low-functioning, as prone to violence and antisocial behaviour.

It is only when the high-functioning, law-abiding, mentally healthy individual commits a crime against a man or woman who is mentally ill that liberals demand extremely tough sentences. In addition, even if the victim is not mentally ill, they may have had a far worse childhood and experienced intense trauma and depression and loss and pain and abandonment, far more so than their attacker, rapist or murderer experienced in their childhood.

No one in a Western nation that has a long tradition of loving dogs, befriending these furry creatures and making them pets, even bringing them into the home with their children, would take pleasure in euthanizing killer dogs who had been responsible for killing their owner or their neighbour's child, no, of course not. No one would desire to hurt the dangerous, mentally unwell and predatory and killer animals, just as no one would take pleasure in euthanizing convicted paedophiles, murderers or terrorists.

Euthanizing a killer dog or a killer man or a killer snake or a killer spider is nothing personal, it is dispassionate and completely non-emotional. Ego and supremacy and sadism and evil are nowhere to be found within capital punishment, nowhere whatsoever, just love, duty and a desire to protect and save the community.

And the difference between a mentally ill killer dog and a mentally ill killer man? The man should have known better. The dog cannot read a list of rules, but men can.

Chapter Twenty-Four—In the Age of Woke, Is It Ever Appropriate to Tell the Enemies of Humanity to Fall on Their Sword?

'I did not know their names. I killed so many women I have a hard time keeping them straight.'
—Gary Ridgway, who murdered at least forty-nine women, mostly sex workers and runaways, whom he lured into his truck and strangled.

(This chapter originally appeared in the book *Wokeism Is Crumbs from the Table of Globalist Elites*)

If you ask me for a list of folk who I believe should have fallen on their sword (either by going into exile or visiting Dignitas in Switzerland) I will be busy for the remainder of the day, thus is the degree of corruption and sleaze that surrounds us in this vain and superficial and greedy little era we live in, with politicians, career criminals, terrorists and rapists and paedophiles being high up on that exhaustive list of undesirable and continually dangerous antisocial and antihuman bottom-feeders, most of whom are sociopaths, psychopaths, narcissists and sadists with no love for humanity, who are motivated solely by self-interest and the multiplication of their own pleasure.

In most nations, it is deemed a crime to encourage suicide, and rightly so as, despite the idiom 'sticks and stones can break my bones but words will never hurt me' providing comfort to some, others take verbal insults or threats or suggestions personally and often act upon them, especially the young and mentally disabled.

Yet, what of unapologetic serial killers? What of unapologetic child killers and rapists and unapologetic terrorists who target and butcher civilians, the most vulnerable and most defenceless victims?

Have we really reached the point where a citizen will be arrested or cancelled or reprimanded for urging killers and rapists and paedophiles and corrupt sleazy politicians to kill themselves, to do the honourable thing of falling on their sword or pulling the lever themselves?

I fear we are approaching this stage, this zenith point of liberal and tolerant madness, which is fertile breeding ground for abusers, for cult leaders, for bad guys, for evildoers as they know that even when they butcher your family, empty your treasury, lay low your morals and culture and take advantage of your kindness and goodwill, you will continue defending them afterwards as you imprison those who encourage bad guys to fall on their swords in order to create balance, in order to prevent the huge cost associated with imprisoning and managing violent sociopaths and violent psychopaths after being convicted of the most gruesome of crimes.

Many Germans and Japanese were found guilty of atrocities and war crimes after WWII, yet upon Germany and Japan surrendering, thousands of gunshots rang out as Germans of all ranks and many of no rank chose to fall on their sword, just as innumerable Japanese men fell on their swords also.

The convicted paedophile who insists that the parents of his victims pay $100,000 per year to house him in prison for the next twenty years before they (and the rest of the people) provide him with accommodation, police protection, healthcare and clothes and furniture and utilities and all the rest is without honour as this is another hurt he is doing unto the flock, which he knows he could prevent by falling on his sword. So we must ask, 'Why don't vile offenders (including corrupt politicians and those who target and abuse the elderly or vulnerable people in general) fall on their swords these days?'

The simple and logical answer is 'because we've got it too good.'

As standards of living have risen, so has the desire of criminals to 'live forever' (including those who cannot be rehabilitated, who will always reoffend, who are devoid of empathy or compassion or love).

In tandem with this, "human rights" is a large factor as when a paedophile, terrorist, rapist, murderer or corrupt politician is faced with twenty years' hard labour with no TV, no creature comforts and forced to share a prison wing with regular folk who have children and who were driven to commit crimes due to need or lack of education, rather than due to greed or sadism or perversion, that person is infinitely more likely to fall on their sword long before they are apprehended for the crime in question.

Currently, when the police announce that they would like to speak to Mr Jenkins about the disappearance of two schoolgirls from Cheshire because he has not been seen in the community for the past week, Mr Jenkins will maybe hide for a few more days or even turn himself in at a police station. Why? Because he will receive free legal help; he will receive his own protected cell on a protected wing of the prison with a TV, heating, a sink and a mirror and a shaver and a rug and newspapers and free dental care, free healthcare, and free medication of all kinds if he desires it and he knows that after his free vacation he will be given a new identity and be protected by the state. He will be given free accommodation and be able to continue hurting people and damaging the fabric of society.

Yet, if Mr Jenkins knew that when caught he would be labouring in a mine, breaking his back for ten hours per day, fed just enough to sustain him, kept in a cell with no window and placed among the general population of the prison who would know 'what he was in for', would he surrender himself to the police and courts? Would Mr Jenkins be happy when he knew he was headed for prison? No. Meaning he would either attempt to flee the country (exile) or he would fall on his sword. Either way, his actions would be deemed to be honourable due to them saving the people untold millions of pounds, euros or dollars over the course of Mr Jenkins' life.

It costs a fortune to pay for Mr Jenkins' prison stay and a fortune to house him after, to watch him, to police him, and a fortune to pay for probation officers and related services and electronic tags and folk to watch Mr Jenkins' location 24/7.

And when Mr Jenkins invariably reoffends, the whole process starts over again, a fortune in court costs, a fortune in prison costs, a fortune in post-prison care in addition to the new mental trauma inflicted upon the community, with victims and relatives of victims seeing their finances affected, lost employment also quite possibly, all so that Mr Jenkins who refuses to fall on his sword can continue doing what he wants to do more than anything—tear society and humanity apart piece by piece.

Bleeding-heart liberals will try to prevent paedophiles and corrupt politicians and terrorists from being introduced into the "normal" parts of the prison, owing to them not wanting real justice to be done as they know these types of sadistic offenders and bullies and perverts will be bullied, attacked and likely killed for their crimes.

Yet the interesting thing about bleeding-heart liberals is they are loved by convicted paedophiles but hated by the victims of paedophiles and terrorists and corrupt politicians, isn't that strange?

And due to liberally minded privileged folk thinking the death penalty barbaric and insisting that paedophiles and killers be protected in prison and kept for life and given new identities all in the interests of extending the lives of those who will never contribute one iota to society, it is necessary to look at new avenues to creating real justice, such as insisting that liberals and only liberals pay for the prison system.

It is obscene, gross, unconscionable to force victims of rape to pay in taxes to house their rapist in a cushy, centrally heated and well lit and comfortable cell with a nice bed and duvet, a big TV, a games console, as much food and snacks as they desire, and healthcare and dental care—this is a crime against the community and against all victims.

If liberals do not have the courage to kill those who can never be rehabilitated, who will never stop killing, who will never stop raping, who will never stop destroying the lives of the innocent, it should of course be privileged liberals and privileged liberals alone who bear the financial burden of protecting, feeding and housing the literal scum of the earth—and when they are released from prison, they should exclusively be housed with bleeding-heart liberals in their homes with them. This is the only way such folk will ever be able to wake up from their fantasy world and delusions of everything being nice, non-triggering and fluffy and no one ever needing to be punished or put to death.

When liberals can no longer afford to go on five holidays per year, when they can only afford a brief staycation once per year as a result of their tax bill doubling overnight as the majority refuse to continue paying tax to fund the lifestyles of the bottom-feeders and detritus of humanity and paedophiles and terrorists and scumbag corrupt politicians, an interesting thing will occur. Their hearts will no longer bleed as they join the land of the sane and rational and responsible and dutiful and strong and proud and resolute, as they demand that unrepentant and unapologetic, cruel and sadistic criminals labour in mines, have no TV, have no view, have no healthcare, have no dental care and receive ZERO police or prison protection from the other prisoners.

And once we reach this natural stage, do you know what will happen? <u>Crime, and thus fear and anxiety and depression and poverty and divorce, will massively reduce.</u>

Rape will go down, murder rates will plummet, terrorism will end, political corruption will cease and thousands of dangerous men and women will suddenly fall on their swords, either by vacating the nation and never returning or by fashioning a noose.

The liberal love and tolerance for the worst criminals causes the worst crimes to occur. This is obvious because as long as there is love and forgiveness and tolerance for criminals (which they mock in secret, thinking liberals deluded and masochistic fools) they will never refrain from hurting people and society and civilisation. However, if the bleeding hearted refuse to pay to house criminals and protect them from the people, criminals everywhere will become massively demotivated to continue their lives of crime.

At this stage, bleeding-heart liberals will say that they, rather than those who desire to swiftly end crime and violence, have the moral high ground, to which I counter with, 'Does that mean you desire a people's referendum on the reintroduction of the death penalty?'

To which they will reply, fascistically, 'No, only enlightened and well-educated liberals should decide what happens rather than the majority of the people.'

We do need that referendum. We need that referendum everywhere, desperately, and we need a referendum on voluntary taxation in regards to funding prison systems across the world. Victims everywhere have had enough. Only elites and the bleeding-heart liberals in our midst should pay to house and protect paedophiles, rapists and murderers and terrorists and corrupt politicians because the vast majority of regular folk desire all of these categories of people to be immediately executed following their conviction.

Chapter Twenty-Five—Pacifists and Anti-Capital Punishment Advocates in a Nutshell

*'Hurry up, you Hoosier b****rd, I could kill ten men while you're fooling around.'*
—Carl Panzram, spoken just before his execution. He claimed to detest the human race and said he would wipe it out if the opportunity arose.

(This chapter originally appeared in the book *Wokeism Is Crumbs from the Table of Globalist Elites*)

The woke, neoliberal, progressive, paedophile-saving and loving, anti-death-penalty citizen in a nutshell. Let's call him David and let's say he lives in Britain.

'David! The enemy have broken through our borders and defences; soon they will reach your house and mine. I am going out to meet them, to either kill them or be killed by them, are you coming to join me?'

'No, I am against violence. I am a pacifist, a conscientious objector. I will not get involved in the defence of my land or my home. The state should do everything for me, other people and classes should do everything for me. I am special and sensitive.'

'So, do you want me to stay in my home? Do you want every man and woman to stay in their home, which will allow the invader to conquer us, one and all?'

'No. If you want to defend me, please do so. If you want to defend our borders, please do so, but I am not going to fight, I do not agree with violence.'

'The problem is, David, the barbarians at the gates very much agree with violence and that 'might is right'. You know, don't you, that if the enemy wins, all of your rights and freedoms, possibly your language and much else will be taken away from you, and if you continue choosing to live on the sidelines, the new bosses will likely throw you into a concentration camp, or worse....'

'I know the stakes, I know that this is a life-or-death struggle, I know danger approaches, but I will not fight, I will not kill, it is as simple as that. These are my unchangeable principles because if I do not want to kill British paedophiles, murderers, rapists and drug dealers, then why would I desire to kill German or Russian or French or Chinese invading soldiers?'

'But you are happy for me to kill any invader on your behalf, to protect you and your children, right?'

'Correct. You can kill if you want, I will not stop you, but I refuse to kill because killing is wrong.'

'David, I am about to risk my life for our collective culture and people, I may die today fighting to keep you free. So please tell me if you want me to kill the invading enemy who has penetrated our borders already. Do you want me to kill the bad guys, yes or no?'

'Okay, it is a yes. I do not want you to surrender, I do not want you to hide or run away. I want you to stand and fight until the death. I want you to save the liberal arts, I want you to fight to save the free press, I want you to fight to save my right to be woke, liberal and a constant contrarian who fights on behalf of criminals and bad guys habitually in peace time.'

'So, you want the invading bad guys to be killed, it is just that you don't want to see the killing, you want to remain in your comfortable, warm home whilst men like me shed blood and fight and kill for you so you can reap all of the rewards afterwards, after all the illiberal, nationalist, unwoke men have died bravely, when all the surplus resources and women will be available to you?

'You wish to be protected like a king but without having to lead, without risking harm coming to yourself. You love your way of life, your liberal, woke, hedonistic and individualistic culture and decadent virtue-signalling life of contrarianism and moral and intellectual supremacy, yet you will not shed a single drop of blood for your culture, nor will you shed a single drop of blood from the invading enemy. If all people like you survive and if all people like me die in this valiant and righteous fight for freedom and sovereignty, what will be the point in fighting? Because within a short period of time, all will become like you, metropolitan liberal elites who wrongly think they are children of the planet, internationalists and entitled to every pleasure and freedom simply by virtue of the fact that you are a human being. I will go now because it is my duty.

'I hate killing, but it is necessary, it is a part of life, and I refuse to surrender to bullies or criminals or invaders, so I will meet the enemy, fight the enemy and one of us will die; but you, David, have surrendered. You should raise a white flag over your house immediately to inform one and all that you are a coward, a parasite and an elitist user who is little more than a fair-weather citizen, a leech, a pest, a destroyer of nations and fidelity and honour and strength and self-sacrifice and community, an internal enemy, a fifth-columnist. Yes, you have surrendered, long before the enemy invaded. You surrendered when you sympathised with rapists and killers and terrorists long ago, when you prevented the return of capital punishment. You are all surrender, all weakness—yet you are my neighbour and my blood, and as selfish and wrong and hypocritical and nation-destroying as you are, a passive-aggressive humanity-hating Batman's Joker hiding in plain sight, I will still fight for you, I will still protect you. I will still die for you.'

Chapter Twenty-Six—What Is Punishment?

*'The women I killed were filth-b****rd prostitutes who were littering the streets. I was just cleaning the place up a bit.'*
—Peter Sutcliffe, the 'Yorkshire Ripper', who took the lives of thirteen women.

(This chapter originally appeared in the book *Wokeism Is Crumbs from the Table of Globalist Elites*)

A man is convicted of a string of serious crimes; the man is a career criminal and almost certain to continue reoffending for the remainder of his life.

He is sentenced to fifteen years in prison.

Upon hearing his sentence pronounced, the convicted man replies, 'No. Thank you for the very generous offer of paying to house and feed and protect and nurture me for the next fifteen years, a fifteen-year-long holiday, but I want to die instead. I want to go to Switzerland where I can legally end my life, which will save taxpayers millions and millions over the course of my life.'

'No. No, you can't be allowed to die!' came the reply.

'But it will cost tax payers 2.3 million dollars over the next fifteen years to keep me in prison and then another few million dollars to house and feed and watch and police me afterwards because I will continue committing crimes for the remainder of my life, if the first half of my life is anything to go by....'

'No, you need to be punished, so you must stay in prison. Your victims prefer to pay taxes to keep you in a nice and comfortable prison in preference to criminals incapable of rehabilitation being euthanized.'

'Am I being punished by being sent to prison or are the taxpayers and my victims being punished? I'm confused.'

'We are very sorry, but this is the system we have. We do not care if it costs five million dollars; we do not care if we have to bankrupt ourselves even, we will not allow you to choose to end your life today in Switzerland. If you wish to legally end your life after you are released from prison that is up to you, but until that time we will be keeping you alive at all costs in prison.'

'But I could end my life tonight in prison if I chose, right?'

'No, wrong—suicide is illegal.'

'But … but I am a criminal, committing crimes is what I do, so calling my suicide illegal is hardly demotivating.'

'In that case, if you are threatening suicide, we will spend extra money sending you to a psychiatric ward where many doctors and specialists and very expensive facilities are to be found, where you will be watched by multiple cameras, watched 24/7 by multiple employees whilst receiving counselling, visits from psychologists and psychiatrists, whist being given various medications. But do not worry; you do not have to pay for any of this, the taxpayer and your victims gladly, proudly pay these bills every time.'

'Can I please ask why you so badly want me alive? You know I'm a rapist and a killer who pushes hard drugs on prepubescent children, right? I'm scum! Why do you want me alive? I am unapologetic! Unapologetic!'

'Because we are anti-capital punishment.'

'We who? And when was the vote? I thought this was a democracy.'

'There was no vote, we just stopped killing killers and traitors and monsters one day because we became liberal and tolerant and bound by this progressive ideology where criminals' lives come first due to our thought leaders being driven by their guilt.'

'Well, if you will not let me legally die today in Switzerland, can we at least have a referendum on the return of capital punishment? Wouldn't you like to see that, Judge?

'No, no, no. The people do not decide the law or the culture or the world outlook of the folk, judges do, and the monarchy and metropolitan liberal elites … and "feelings". The feelings and emotions of the very important privileged few decide the fate of the many.'

'So, let me understand this. Elites spared my life because they feel guilty that they are on the top and I'm on the bottom?'

'Yes.'

'But elites also encourage my reoffending, don't they, due to knowing the rope or guillotine would be hugely demotivating to people like me? If I knew I could lose my life, do you think I would snatch bags and deal drugs? Of course not.'

'We understand your position and we do sympathise, yet the system in place requires you to have a vacation now. You will now be forced into retirement for fifteen years. You are forced to rest, to become inactive and depressed and apathetic as you develop an ever greater hatred for society and the nation and for police and judges and for the law-abiding many.

'You see, if you do not go to prison lots of people will lose their jobs, from prison guards to those who build and maintain prisons, to those who sell food, clothing and similar goods to prisons to be used by prisoners, and of course, upon release you would encounter probation officers and folk who fit electronic tags. All of these people too would lose their employment if killers and rapists and traitors and corrupt politicians all simply killed themselves rather than putting their feet up in a comfortable, protected hotel room for a decade or two.'

'Forgive me if I am speaking out of turn here, but it seems that if you want to protect regular people, the first place to start would be at the treasury—what good is there in keeping me in prison for fifteen years or fifty years if that act bankrupts all of my victims? They are now being hurt in a different way, yet I am causing the hurt because I choose to stay alive and exist in a parasitical way, leeching off the hosts and community I have attacked and abused. But I wish to die; I wish to visit the clinic in Switzerland where legal euthanasia is possible. I will keep offending, it will cost a fortune to keep me for the next sixty years, or even the next hundred and twenty years what with scientific advances and ever more socialised medicine and free healthcare—free for me but not for my victims....'

'There is nothing more to say, elites have decided your fate. You will remain in prison. If you try to hurt or kill yourself we will intervene, whatever the financial cost may be, and taxes will continue to be raised again and again moving forward as others are similarly imprisoned for lengthy periods at great expense and burden to the people. Again, this is the will of those who make the law.'

'A final thing, Judge; during my trial you scolded me for stealing $1000 from one of my victims because she was working three jobs at the time and struggling to save enough money to fix her car. Why do you think it is that she was working those three jobs in the first place and why do you think it is that she couldn't afford to fix her car? Taxes, because of high taxes, because of people like me. And her taxes will rise again now because you insist on keeping this bizarre, unnatural system alive, and me alive also, which is illogical, which evidences your self-abnegation and masochism. I will keep hurting you, so why are you continually kind to me? Are you mad?'

'No, we are kind, tolerant, forgiving, liberal and progressive citizens who want everyone to be happy and alive for as long as humanly possible without exceptions, and yes, I did scold you for taking that $1000, but I will not scold you for now costing taxpayers that $2.3 million you mentioned earlier, which is what it will cost to keep you locked up for fifteen years, because taxpayers insist they spend that money. They choose to spend that money on you, so it is not your fault, the blame is not yours.'

'Who is to blame, then, for higher taxes, recidivism, antisocial behaviour, disorder, and huge national debt?'

'The citizens of course. These things are the fault of regular taxpayers who have the right and ability to vote for anyone they want yet they continually vote for the anti-death-penalty candidate and ever-higher-taxes candidate, which is why they cannot complain about the high taxes; which is why you cannot be allowed to visit Switzerland.'

Guards appear in the court, they begin removing the convicted criminal, taking him to prison.

'Judge, one last thing: If I promise to kill you, your family, the entire jury and every child under five years old in this town, will you still release me once again?'

'No. If you pose a danger to the public, the public will continue paying to keep you in prison.'

'Okay. I understand everything now. If I want a hard life of searching for work, maintaining a house and land, running a car and remembering to pay the tax and insurance and to service it also, maintaining good relations with neighbours, paying my utility bills, ironing and washing my clothes and paying for my healthcare and food what I need to do is announce that I am a changed man in fifteen years, born again, seen the light, rehabilitated.

'Yet, if I do not wish to do all that hard work and burden myself with all of that stress, all I need to do is threaten people and those very same people will reach into their pockets, pull out the fruits of their labours and shower me with money, free food, free utilities, electricity for life guaranteed, always running water, free dental care and healthcare, TVs and toiletries and never a bill in sight, never, ever, ever, ever. If I'm a bad guy, an evil guy, you will give me millions and a great lifestyle. What is wrong with you, seriously? What the hell is wrong with you?'

Chapter Twenty-Seven—The Opt-In Taxation Form

'I was born with the devil in me. I could not help the fact that I was a murderer, no more than the poet can help the inspiration to sing.'
—H. H. Holmes, who confessed to twenty-seven murders. He designed a three-storey building complete with trapdoors, airtight rooms and a basement to dispose of the bodies of the young women he lured inside.

(This chapter originally appeared in the book *Make America United Again: The Trump-Harris Co-Presidency 2024 – 2028*)

A sample Opt-In Taxation (voluntary taxation) form:

Place a tick in the boxes below if you wish to opt in to pay higher taxes to fund some of, or all of, the departments, institutions or causes below:

Prisons [ ]
Probation Service [ ]
Socialised Medicine [ ]
Welfare [ ]
Border Security/Military [ ]
Foreign Aid [ ]
Refugee Causes/Immigration [ ]
Space Programs/Space Colonisation [ ]
Abortion [ ]

Imagine being presented with such a form, which would of course include multiple additional choices. Imagine being able to choose exactly where and how the fruits of your hard labours are spent.

If you desire the nation to become defenceless whilst only convicted killers, rapists and refugees financially benefit from your taxes, you will have the ability to pay taxes to fund certain agendas and certain government departments—but only *you* should pay for what *you* want. Others should not be forced to agree with you or forced to pay to help you get what you want if they fundamentally disagree with you.

If you have debts, are poor and cannot afford to pay for any of the things above, you will only opt in to help fund these things if you are lost to masochism, self-harm or are the victim of extreme cultish indoctrination and self-hatred.

If you are wealthy and care about the security of your community and nation, you will of course fund the protection and defence of your nation, which begins with good stout borders and a tenacious and undefeatable military.

If you are liberally minded and hyper-empathic and driven by tolerance and forgiveness and affirmative actions and "social justice", of course you will be permitted to fund the departments and projects that are closest to your heart, irrespective of how much hurt all this giving causes to your wallet. Of course you will be permitted to share the fruits of your labours with foreign people, foreign nations and foreign causes if that is your desire, and of course you will also be able to fund other people's healthcare (at home and abroad), other people's housing (at home and abroad) and other people's food bills and utilities (at home and abroad) if that is important to you.

Opt-In Taxation is a quantum leap forward for democracy, people power and transparency and equality. Why should the liberal 'One Worlder' be forced to pay for a military and border wall he loathes?

Why should a nationalist be forced to pay for foreign causes, refugees and foreign aid?

Why should the victim of rape be forced to fund her rapist's stay in prison and afterwards his rehousing in her community and probation and all the rest of it?

If you have deep pockets and deep guilt, give, opt in and thus fund the life extension of paedophiles, terrorists and unrepentant killers and violent bullies. If you have deep pockets and deep guilt, opt in and thus fund the life extension of those who choose to smoke, choose to drink alcohol, choose to eat to excess and as a result have all developed killer diseases and illnesses that require millions to be spent on them and millions more to be spent in welfare and housing and assorted healthcare bills.

If you personally or you as a business or corporation desire to pay to extend the lives of folk who have disabled themselves, who have injured themselves, who, rather than saving money to one day be able to afford medical treatment, spent that money on holidays and cigarettes, drugs and vanity tech, fashion trends and gambling, go ahead, no one will stop you. Please give as much as you desire to these categories of folk; but do not expect nor attempt to compel the rest of society to similarly join in with your self-sacrifice.

No more free healthcare and no more free welfare will cause millions to spit out poisonous cigarettes and flush toxic whiskey down the toilet as houses are got back into order and folk grow up, lose the weight, throw the junk food away and start digging for victory once more.

Opt-In is not punishment; rather, it is an equality-birthing and motivating and inspiring means to save our peoples and communities from an abysmal existence of shared suffering, failure, defeat, apathy, surrender and living far, far, far beyond one's own means.

Chapter Twenty-Eight—Desert Islands Kill Woke Ideology Every Time, Guaranteed

'Assassin? That sounds so exotic, I was just a murderer.'
—Richard Kuklinski, who was convicted of five murders but claimed to have committed over two hundred with increasingly elaborate murder methods such as poisoning, immolation and feeding his victims to rats.

(This chapter originally appeared in the book *Wokeing Kills*)

The vacation of a lifetime, a round-the-world luxury cruise, was brought to a sudden halt for recently divorced Kate McCafferty and her daughter when disaster struck in the middle of the night. No one knew quite what happened; all Kate knew was she was shipwrecked with her only child. Two unlikely survivors of the tragedy that saw the huge vessel disappear under the calm, moonlit ocean were washed up, Tom Hanks style, on a desert island.

It was a miracle, but as Kate saw no sign of civilisation or other survivors, she guessed she and Tess, her daughter, stood very little chance of ever being found....

As bleak as the situation seemed, and as demotivating as the situation was, Kate couldn't think of herself, of self-pity, of wallowing in the tragedy and the great human loss or thinking about her being lonely, detached from her social circles and the internet, far from Starbucks and credit cards and traffic and makeup and the woke and BLM marches she enthusiastically attended and all the rest of it from 'back home'. All she could think about in that precise moment was Tess, was saving Tess.

The island the two survivors found themselves stranded upon was expansive, around the size of fifty football fields Kate guessed after swimming out a few hundred metres in the ocean in order to get a better view of the island in full.

It soon became apparent also that the island had adequate clean drinking water, arable land, and there were wild fruits and vegetables, which the two could eat and replant in order to be able to survive long-term. There were also waters rich in fish and other types of seafood; there were several fishing nets washed up on the beach. It would be easy to begin catching fish and to collect water and a few coconuts and berries.

Mother and daughter had been at sea for many hours, floating precariously on various pieces of luggage and holidaymakers' suitcases as they drifted and drifted, sent miles away as waves pushed them further and further into the middle of nowhere—which told Kate the pair might not be rescued any time soon. Immediately her priorities shifted and she no longer felt as though she needed help as help was not there, it was not forthcoming. She did not become stronger or more courageous as she began planning the long-term survival of her family; rather, the strength and courage and will to dauntlessly survive anything and everything was always there, only now unlocked at this greatest hour of need imaginable, after being buffeted by Poseidon, after being torn out of consumerist and addiction and service industry, debt-centred modernity. Kate knew she would survive, she was in no doubt; she had been reborn, baptised in purpose. She relished the challenge and the growth she and her daughter would experience now that they were able to recuperate from the culture wars, peer pressure, political correctness, groupthink and enforced conformity that had suffocated and petrified the pair in equal measure, despite the smiles they sported when being 're-educated'.

The world will think we went down with everyone else and with the ship. I cannot rely on others; I cannot rely on the state. I must stand alone, for Tess. I will be strong for her, I will protect her.

***

Kate hurriedly made a shelter out of leaves and small tree branches to keep the baking sun off her and her child's backs; by the first night the shelter was complete and the two had achieved the feat together and afterwards bonded under the stars, far from internet or radio or TV signals or the noise of the city and of capitalism and consumerism and fast-paced globalisation, stock markets and constant international travel and trade and movement. Life was hell without these things for Kate, so used to them and addicted to them as she was, but life was bliss without them also—and a remarkable thing then happened. Kate began thinking for herself because there were no voices instructing her and directing her will and charity-giving and support of every cause and gripe on planet Earth.

The next morning, she awoke with optimism in her heart, confident about being able to tame the island, construct more buildings, and collect more food—and then *he* arrived, another survivor, who announced to Kate on the beach that he had been adrift at sea for twenty hours or more, that he too was aboard the same ship. He seemed very happy to see Kate and her child.

The island Kate was marooned upon was one in a chain of islands, with her island being the smallest but easily capable of sustaining her and Tess for many years to come.

'Would you mind if I came to join you here?' the stranger asked. 'Or I could visit one of the other islands if you want to be left alone, if you are happy to be independent and prefer to be separate. There are other islands; I can take one of those. It is your decision.' As he spoke he floated effortlessly in the ocean due to being adorned in not one but three life jackets and was able to propel and manoeuvre himself via the use of a single oar, which seemed to have come from a canoe Kate thought, looking upon the strange scene, still weary from the previous day's trials, privations and exertions.

Kate now had a choice.

She could invite this man, this stranger, to live with her and her daughter merely because he was a human who would likely prefer company and the help of others than being alone.

In the past Kate would have said no to the man due to her long caring about herself and her survival, about keeping her community peaceful, calm and well ordered; after all, there were other islands not all that far away, he could have reached them within ten minutes of paddling, no great hardship. Yet, in recent years Kate had encountered wokeism; she was influenced by the pop stars and celebrities on the television and the internet she became addicted to after going out in their local town became too dangerous due to the rising violent crime levels that followed the election of the liberal and forgiving politician in that area.

Since becoming woke, since agreeing for responsibility and duty to be shifted to the state in exchange for her obedience and willingness to pay ever higher taxes to the ideologues who came to guide and puppeteer her, Kate no longer became angry or scared when she heard the news reports about girls or women being abused or even murdered in her country because this terrible news, this terrible reality made possible by liberalism, which ensures rising crime rates and recidivism, served to be a relief for Kate and woke liberal women like her. They were relieved that it was not them or their daughters or friends or relatives who were victimised by the evil forces tolerated and forgiven by progressive woke liberalism, a pseudo religion, a pseudo cult that demands strict adherence and tolerates no competition. This book may be banned here, there and everywhere if wokeists get their way, no doubt—but they're not fascists ... really!

Kate was educated, or re-educated, by the woke ideology and religion in how she should react to news of paedophilia and imported terrorism, political corruption, nepotism, misconduct in public office and a myriad of other crimes and offences. This knowledge became known to her through groupthink, social media and peer pressure, with influencers among the woke folk feeding down their will and vision and it being lapped up by those below, keen to impress the head girls and boys, keen to prove their virtuousness and goodness and purity....

Kate knew that she should never, under any circumstances, as a progressive and wise, loving and caring and intelligent and woke liberal show visible signs of anger when hearing about violent and sexual crimes, even when hearing news about children being killed. Wokeists are expected to remain unmoved, reacting in an unnatural, inhuman way, a robotic and cold way.

Kate also knew that she should never loudly advocate for the victim or spend any amount of time raising awareness of that type of crime in her local area; as in, when she saw on the news that a rapist had struck again near her child's school, she responded by turning the news off and spending two hours worrying that the rapist was being bullied in prison by evil, misogynist, patriarchal dinosaurs.

She was programmed, well trained, docile, servile and enfeebled; she was made into a lamb to the slaughter. Big tech loved her, pimps loved her, big capitalism loved her and the big banks loved her—because she gave so much away to people who were the opposite of her in all ways that she constantly needed to take out additional credit to fund her woke extravagances and woke hedonistic, self-abnegating excesses.

Kate was happy being controlled and dominated. It did not matter to her whether it was an ideology or religion or a fringe political group or cause—all that mattered was that she was accepted; she felt protected and strong within the guilt-rich circle of vulnerable people hoping and praying they made the right decision when they threw their lot in with wokeism and liberalism. But could they truly believe this divisive ideology could solve all their problems, even the problems in their own private lives?

By surrendering her voice, freedom of speech and individuality to the state via immersion in woke orthodoxy, which is tolerated by foolish suicidal states and actively encouraged by failed states, Kate had received cast-iron job protection with her woke liberal identity opening doors and keeping those doors open. In the era of liberal cancel culture, you either get woke, surrender and receive protection/exemption or remain an individual and ask to have civil and calm debates about the issues and eventually become blacklisted and bullied.

Was Kate a victim? Was she an enthusiastic follower? Was she 'only following orders' when she engaged in woke mob tactics and radical pressure campaigns that involved blackmail and the use of violence and anarchy? It matters not how she came to become woke or what her true motivations were for choosing the government-supported mainstream academic liberal doctrine over all others. All that mattered was she was woke enough on that day on that desert island to say 'yes' to the man when 'no' would have been so much easier and would have made so much more sense.

Kate agreed for the man to move to their island.

She shared some of her food with the man and helped him build a shelter.

The next day, Kate was taking the man's coat to him, which he had left near to her modest dwelling, when a news article fell out of the pocket, which had been cut out of a newspaper a few days prior.

Reading it, she saw the terrible truth that the man she had helped and planned to continue to help was a convicted paedophile. It was unmistakable; that was Tom in the photo and he had served three years for crimes against children.

Normally, back in the fantasy world where there is the nanny state and credit and millions of shops and folk who are ready and willing to work for you, service you and help you in a myriad of ways, Kate would not have grimaced at learning a man was a paedophile, thus was her high rank within the woke intellectual hierarchy. Yet something was different now, something was wrong. She felt odd, out of sorts, and not at all like her usual woke, liberal, progressive, tolerant, self-abnegating, pro-criminal-rehabilitation self.

'If that filth goes near my child I will gut him like a fish!' the woke vegan pacifist found herself gutturally muttering under her breath as she saw Tom waving at her young child.

In a flash, the woke ideology vanished as natural instinct, love and loyalty, honour, duty and true sacrifice came to the fore as Kate became one thousand times stronger and wiser and more capable in every regard, until she remembered one liberal lesson she had been taught about victims of childhood bullying going on to be bullies and criminals themselves, the point being that everyone is blameless. That was what Kate was taught, that we should never stand up for ourselves and never fight back or kill bullies, attackers or rapists because 'it's not their fault.'

This echo of woke domination, guilt-tripping, gaslighting, psychological manipulation and intense unnatural conditioning wrestled control back from her, preventing nature from bringing about a resolution, as when the wokeism rose up again within Kate, she dutifully retook her psychologically subservient position as she psychologically sat, gave a psychological paw, dwelt on everything bad or less than perfect about herself and also dwelt on the fact that paedophiles are someone's child too and they have feelings and don't like being sad....

Hurriedly, Kate put away the news article and didn't think to ask herself why this man was carrying such a thing around with him, risking his secret coming to light by others stumbling upon it.

'Tom, your coat is here. I will leave it on the beach for you. You don't want to get cold; we are a long way from a hospital.' Kate decided to react in the woke liberal way. She decided to do nothing, to surrender and to risk herself and her daughter coming to serious harm in the coming anxiety-filled woke paradise days with the omnipresent threat posed by Tom, the man Kate foolishly invited into her home and helped, because that was the woke and nice thing to do, and was now happy to continue living alongside of, despite knowing he was dangerous. He had proven he was dangerous and Kate also knew that this man chose to put himself on their island, an island where a child lived, rather than keeping himself separate from them.

That evening, Kate saw Tom dancing with her young child. At the time, she smiled (a fake smile), just as she had smiled when two bearded drag queens performed their risqué and grown-up act for her child's class at their school for some bizarre reason (likely hurting and embarrassing Daddy). However, later, after she had put her child to bed, Kate asked Tom to meet her on the beach, saying she needed to discuss something.

'I know, Tom. I know about your past, so back off. Maybe you should view the other islands after all.'

'No. I may have injured my leg today; I will need to stay a while.'

No he didn't, he didn't hurt his leg today, Kate thought, surveying the man very carefully up and down as if he were a lion about to leap in her direction, teeth bared. *That limp has only developed within the last few seconds—the liar, the deceiver!*

'I might need you to do my chores for the next few days in fact, until I am better again, stronger. So no, I don't think I will be going anywhere anytime soon and the real crime here is you invading my privacy.'

Speechless and dumbfounded by the man's gaslighting, bravado and insistence upon remaining on the island with the woman and child, Kate murmured weakly, 'Okay,' before retiring to her makeshift dwelling. Tom smiled as he witnessed the sight and what he took to be liberal woke surrender as he was already planning to attack her or her daughter whilst they slept. But Kate did not plan to sleep, far from it.

***

Tess awoke after midday, not that time, hours and minutes were of much use in that far-flung isolated place. The young girl was exhausted both psychologically and mentally; the rest had done her good, yet she awoke with an incredible hunger. 'Ouch,' she blurted, feeling the discomfort of being hungry and in need of food for the first time in her life.

'Mum? Mum, where are you? I'm hungry. What are we going to eat, Mum? Mum?'

As Tess repeated her questions somewhat louder, a response came back from just behind the line of coconut trees leading to the beach. 'Here, darling. All is well now; there is nothing to worry about. I'm just making breakfast.'

Tess took in the sight of her mild-mannered liberal vegan mother casting a huge net into the ocean as she stood in the sea up to her waist; to Tess's eyes it appeared as though her mother had been catching fish and hunting and gathering her entire life. She felt a rush of pride flow through her, but it was followed by confusion and she blurted out, 'But the fish's feelings ... veganism....'

'Those things are for the old world, they are a privilege and a luxury that we cannot afford in this natural place. We want to survive, yes? Veganism is gone; woke is gone. Compassion for anything or anyone else needs to end immediately, Tess. We must just focus on being strong and motivated, happy and healthy. Whatever it takes we will survive, we can do this.'

'Yes, okay, the diets and mourning for everyone and thinking about all other suffering need to go away,' a very hungry young Tess replied as her eyes witnessed three fish enter her mother's net, eliciting a guttural 'Eureka!' from a determined Kate who in that moment might as well have been standing atop a mountain as she bravely battled sabre-toothed tigers in order to protect her treasured child mid ice age with her unbeatable proud ancestors, the apex of every species, the best of the best of the best, the most deserving and noble and glorious, a tribute to creation.

'And Tom, where's Tom?'

'He needed to go away too,' Kate coldly told Tess, not making eye contact with her. 'Maybe he will return one day, but I think he needs to be on his own, three's a crowd and all that....'

Tess's first thought was that there would be more food, more space and more resources to go around now that Tom had seemingly gone AWOL whilst she slept. She was oblivious to what had occurred, what had to occur.

Years later, Tess would be told the truth of Tom's departure, which explained the mother and daughter suddenly having three life vests in their inventory.

Kate had returned to the beach some minutes after pretending to retire to bed. Tom did not see or hear her approach as she walked barefoot on the island's white sandy beach as she ducked low, gathering up two of the larger coconuts that had fallen from above.

She swung the coconut she held in her left palm as hard as she possibly could in a roundhouse motion as she gritted her teeth and thought only of her daughter's survival and her dignity remaining intact. She violently connected with Tom's temple, rocking him, almost knocking him to the ground. Kate saw his angered expression as he staggered back attempting to remain on his feet; then she sent the second coconut in his direction, swinging it as hard and mightily as possible, it hurtling towards his left temple as she swung her right arm with all her might, summoning unknown strength and willpower. Tom fell down dead. Kate buried him as Tess slept.

After eating their late breakfast of fish and crab, the two spent the entire day together, sitting around their campfire, with Kate's arm wrapped protectively around her ward as she felt relieved and in shock about what had happened, about what she had been forced to do, and the fact that her child was still alive, healthy, happy and singing songs around the fire, which caused Kate to cry tears of unbridled joy, a welcome departure from her former depressed and angered cynical woke "normal".

'Do you think we will ever be rescued, Mummy?'

We already have been, Tess. We already have been, Kate thought, smiling.

***

The Next Day

Kate and Tess were snapped out of their berry-and-firewood-hunting mission when they heard a man's voice boom out to them.

'It's Tom, he's come back. Maybe he will show us some more dance moves, eh?' Tess innocently blurted out, believing he had returned. Kate's eyes widened as the hairs on the back of her neck stood up in tandem with the clenching of her right fist.

The man shouted again as he came into view approaching through the dense forest. 'I am a survivor of a shipwreck; I've been drifting at sea for days. Hello? Is there anyone here?'

Before Kate could place a hand over Tess's mouth or instruct her to be cautious when encountering strangers, the young girl shouted out, 'We are shipwrecked too. Here, we are over here!'

It immediately became apparent that the voice belonged to a newcomer, rather than Tom.

Kate sent Tess away, telling her to check the beach for new washed-up debris, fishing nets and anything of general use. She gave her instructions in the form of a challenge, which set Tess off running, thinking of impressing her mother and the newcomer. 'You can trust me,' she insisted. 'I will be back in ten with so many goodies. You two wait here.'

Kate's normal exterior – the people-pleasing, fake-smiling, makeup-rich, facetious exterior – was gone after the trauma of the ship going down, the time at sea, building, hunting, fighting to survive and battling dangerous, unrepentant rapists. She greeted the stranger with an expressionless face, a face of stoicism and strength, which demanded respect. Somehow Kate knew to be this way, it suited her and caused the man to offer his hand to shake hers, rather than embrace her, rather than hug her or kiss her. She kept him at arm's length, literally.

He told of how he was a passenger, that he was a survivor like her and Tess and that he was so glad to have washed up on their island as he loved people and company and hated being on his own because he claimed to have been an orphan. 'That's why I go on cruises you see, because it feels like I have family then. I travel alone, but it feels like I am on a family excursion when I am on a cruise ship.'

Just a few days ago Kate would have been welling up as emotional empathy and people-pleasing compassion overtook her, as she reached for the Kleenex against her conscious will, moved to tears and emotion despite not wishing to be. Yet after the events of yesterday she merely nodded, acknowledging she had heard the man's words and nothing more, as she sought to maintain her emotional sovereignty, her control over her emotions and instincts and will, as being in control and being able to lead herself and her family was important now, was imperative, Kate felt, for the collective survival of her family, of humanity, of love and of hope.

Due to her demeanour, the newcomer knew not to get too close to her or her daughter; he instead spent most of his time alone, only visiting them when he wanted to eat or when he needed help building a shelter or fishing.

Weeks passed and the island remained calm with a burning anxiety filling Kate's heart, which she forced down as she constructed weapons, moved the family's dwelling to a more protected location and remained vigilant, until she overheard the newcomer talking to himself as she brought him a couple of coconuts for his lunch.

'They will think I went down with the ship. They will think I am a victim. There will be a funeral for me and the fools will be crying and mourning, never knowing that I was the one, I was the mastermind who caused the fuel tanks to explode in the engine room tearing the hull. The fools will never know that I killed those three thousand people, men, women and children....'

As the man finished his sentence, his eyes became deranged, manic; his pupils dilated as he paced back and forth and his head twitched uncontrollably. Kate rushed forward, armed with the two coconuts. Her aim was true; she won justice for the fallen whilst safeguarding her family.

'I will never be a victim again!' she screamed after removing the threat, after doing her duty as a Homo sapien.

Chapter Twenty-Nine—How Woke Creates Hell on Earth

'I ought to have been hanged. I deserved it. My crime was worse than Brady's because I enticed the children and they would never have entered the car without my role... I have always regarded myself as worse than Brady.'

—Myra Hindley, convicted of three counts of murder and referred to by the press as 'the most evil woman in Britain.'

(This chapter originally appeared in the book *Wokeism Is Crumbs from the Table of Globalist Elites*)

Two serial killers (who were also convicted and self-confessed paedophiles) were released from prison after completing their sentence, one male, one female, both wishing to live together, both wishing to start a life together, to produce children together....

The vast majority of people in the nation would have preferred it if these two predators and dangers to everyone's children were no longer alive, with most desiring a referendum on capital punishment; yet many feared radical liberal progressives calling them "evil" and "fascist" so instead, under great pressure, continued to remain silent and 'on script' as fascists were hung after the Nuremburg Trials. In a pre-woke era, we called bad guys fascists; now we call those who desire serial killers and paedophiles to be legally executed fascists, what a state of affairs.

The few, only the very few troubled souls in our midst, desired these two rapist killers to be released. I use the term rapist killers rather than humans because they were not human in the traditional sense as they thought only of their own pleasure, and they would only ever think of their own pleasure and would continue hurting, destroying and torturing people and society until the moment their hearts stopped beating.

Wolves are great, aren't they? So majestic and beautiful. Yet would you release a wolf into your small community or allow one to walk around stores and malls and shopping centres where children are present?

No.

Why?

Because, just like paedophiles, rapists and sadistic human monsters lacking empathy in general, wolves are incredibly dangerous, so despite all wolves having mothers, we cannot allow them to live alongside us, ever.

No one, other than the most committed (deluded) wokevists who have chosen woke as their eternal excuse for not getting their house in order, would actually want these two scumbags to get married, to live together and to begin producing children together … but that is exactly what happened due to these predators residing in a tolerant and forgiving liberal democracy.

A woke liberal priest married the Myra Hindley and Ian Brady-esque pair almost immediately following their release.

The tolerant liberal state gave them a house for free and new identities, new lives, a car to get about in and enough help, money and support to allow them to create a life together and to create new lives together— babies.

The tolerant liberal and masochistic state then provided free healthcare to the pair and aided them throughout the first, second, third and fourth pregnancies.

The two paedophiles received the blessing of the woke priest, the woke probation officers, the woke judges, the woke parole board, the woke welfare system, woke politicians and the woke socialised medical establishment that enabled their every want to be satisfied.

Soon the family was huge; yet, of course, neither convicted serial killer rapist could ever work again (due to their notoriety and infamy) and they had to be kept by regular folk for the remainder of their lives as normal, healthy-minded, critical-thinking and decent folk soon began to worry terribly about the fate of the children now in the care of the monsters who previously destroyed so many lives, who still refused to say just how many people they abused and killed.

The children were not told their parents' real identities, which imperilled them.

The children could not receive a normal upbringing and did not receive genuine or natural nurture or education due to being home-schooled by two convicted serial killers.

The only ones to benefit from this mad, perverse arrangement were the two paedophile killers and the wokeists who virtuously and benevolently agreed to all their demands and agreed also to bankrupt themselves to advantage the serial-killing paedophiles whilst creating certain perils ahead by giving two evil-doers everything they wanted again and again and again.

***

This is not a civil liberties issue, this is not about what the law says is permitted. No community, society or nation that wishes to long survive can ever tolerate convicted rapists, paedophiles, serial killers or terrorists freely associating with one another following release from prison, living together or breeding. This is masochism, unimaginable masochism, and self-sabotage all for the sake of a poorly conceived ideology birthed in the mind of hate-and-envy-filled fifth-columnists and folk such as the disgraced William Quilliam, the grandfather of woke.

***

A male serial killer, paedophile and lifelong enemy of civilisation is released from prison by loving and compassionate, bleeding-hearted liberal woke folk.

A female serial killer, paedophile and lifelong enemy of civilisation is released from prison by loving and compassionate, bleeding-hearted liberal woke folk.

How I would react to the dual conviction of the two individuals:

I would request that both of the paedophile murderers were legally executed following a referendum on the subject of euthanasia for murderers, paedophiles, rapists, corrupt politicians, fifth-columnists, spies, terrorists and traitors.

The cost? Two lengths of rope.

How wokeists would react to the dual conviction of the two individuals:

- Woke liberals would demand the rapist killers were provided protection in prison, even if that meant endangering the lives of the guards who were forced to put themselves in harm's way when the regular prisoners (of course) continually attempted to kill the rapist killers.

- Woke liberals would request that both convicted rapists and murderers were given new identities to protect them upon release. The cost? Millions.

- Woke liberals would request that both individuals be given a free house, free healthcare, free food, free utilities, free clothes and free police protection, likely a vehicle for free also, with the two likely being unable to get normal jobs. The cost? Millions.

Chapter Thirty—If Jesus Was Without Sin, Why Didn't He Cast the First Stone?

'We do whatever we enjoy doing. Whether it happens to be judged good or evil is a matter for others to decide.'
—Ian Brady, 'Moors Murderer', convicted of killing five children between the ages of ten and seventeen and sexually assaulting at least four of them.

The 'do not cast the first stone' parable is intended to prevent the people being able to exert judgement and control, with Jesus no doubt intervening at the Nuremberg Trials (if in attendance) when the architects of the Third Reich were sentenced to death, stating to the judges, 'Are you all without sin? No! Which means you cannot hurt these people, you must release them immediately!'

The problem with this 'don't get justice, don't ensure there's a strict deterrent in place to dissuade psychopaths from destroying the fabric of society' parable is that it protects serial killers, traitors, spies, fifth-columnists, paedophiles and men who sell heroin and fentanyl to children.

If one of the people holding large killer stones in their hands had offered their stone to Jesus, would he have thrown it at the intended victim?

No.

It seems certain that Jesus would have dropped the stone upon the ground rather than casting it in anger because the very Disney version of reality created by parables such as this have no place for violence or blood or gore or justice or tumult or disagreement or stress or anything else that is real and necessary.

Jesus would have dropped the stone.

Everyone would have asked if that meant he was a sinner.

Jesus would likely have said, 'No, I am not a sinner.'

To which everyone would have replied, 'But you said only sinners were prevented from casting stones.'

To which Jesus would have replied, 'I don't want anyone to cast stones; I don't want anyone to be punished for anything. Instant forgiveness every time is what I preach.'

'So,' they would have replied, 'you are saying that because even you, who are sinless, would not cast a stone, it means that we are not responsible for the crimes and sin of this person here, that they chose to break laws and Commandments? It's just that you don't want them to come to harm in any way as a result because you prefer anarchy over order?'

At this point, Jesus would be forced to backtrack on his 'he who is without sin' excuse for forgiving all wrongdoing, crimes and transgressions and instead devise a new excuse (cognitive dissonance) for a liberal woke 'Disney' reality to be created ... or he could just magic free food and free wine into existence in order to bribe people if guilt-tripping and 'original sin' is found not to be enough to cause folk to become passive and tolerant of everything, all the time, even the worst transgressions and crimes imaginable.

Chapter Thirty-One—Leaders Are Never Pacifists or Anti-Capital Punishment

'I like killing people because it is so much fun. It is more fun than killing wild game in the forest because man is the most dangerous animal of them all.'
—The Zodiac Killer, who claimed responsibility for at least five people in 1968–1969. He wrote many letters to local newspapers, one of which contained the quote above.

(This chapter originally appeared in the book *Wokeism Is Crumbs from the Table of Globalist Elites*)

A candidate for political office may declare themselves a pacifist, liberal, tolerant and completely opposed to capital punishment, even for unrepentant serial killers, terrorists and traitors, but a leader, a leader of a new community never could, as is evidenced in the following scenario.

You are one of two hundred survivors of a shipwreck.

You and the other 199 people find sanctuary on a small island, barely large enough to house and sustain the survivors, who are from different cultures, classes and nations.

If you are liberal and what was referred to as 'woke' during the first half of the 21st century, your attempt at leadership of this group, so far from home, unlikely to ever be found due to being in the middle of nowhere, the middle of an ocean, would look something like this:

You tell the other 199 people that, if they follow you, they can choose to fish if they want to fish as part of a community effort to provide food and resources to the tribe, but if they do not want to kill, or do not want to work, they will be fed anyway.

You tell the other 199 people that, if they follow you, they will be invited to build structures, housing and signal fires, but if they do not want to do these things, if they prefer to rest in the shade for whatever reason, they can still benefit from the hard work and labours undertaken by the other members of the tribe.

You tell the other 199 people that, if they follow you, there will exist a liberal and hedonistic 'free society' on the island, whereby everyone's individual belief system and religion and philosophy and point of view are treated equally are given parity and all considered valid, even if you believe in ghosts and UFOs and alien abductions and the entire world being part of an elaborate technological computer simulation—and even Satanists are told they can loudly and proudly 'practise their faith' on the main beach where most folk communally gather to relax and socialise.

You tell the other 199 people also that, if they follow you, free love will reign supreme, stating that if anyone wishes to produce children on the tiny island, they can; you also state that you do not wish for there to be an age of consent.

You tell the other 199 people also that, if they follow you, there will be no police, no jails, no rules or laws of any kind, that all people will be considered to be sovereign spiritual beings deserving of infinite tolerance and love and happiness regardless of what they do and how they behave towards the other members of the tribe.

If, however, you are illiberal and unwoke, your leadership style would be completely different; it would look something like this:

You tell the other 199 people that, if they follow you, they will each be protected from bullies, rapists, muggers, violent sociopaths, dangerous psychopaths and dishonourable work-shirking parasites who wish to live like kings whilst all others toil and work hard.

You tell the other 199 people that, if they follow you, there will immediately be written a charter, with there being introduced sensible rules which, when followed by all, create identity, cohesion, continuity, stability, order and peace.

You tell the other 199 people that, if they follow you, you will get them off the island or die trying, that you care not for their momentary fleeting happiness as you insist no children are birthed on the very small island (which can barely sustain the 200 survivors), knowing that a sudden overpopulation would lead to civil strife, and due to the absence of medical professionals, abortions would be impossible and safe pregnancies would be difficult to achieve also.

You tell the other 199 people that, if they follow you, you will ensure that members of the small tribe who are raped, bullied or killed will not be ignored and forgotten, as would have been the case under liberal, hedonistic, pacifistic leadership, but rather, these folk will become martyrs, their names entering songs, their likenesses carved into rocks, their memories kept alive in the new system of law and order that you would introduce to the small island nation. You would guarantee justice, swift and fair justice, with all being judged the same, be the offender rich, poor, black, white, male, female, low-functioning, high-functioning, mentally ill or mentally healthy.

You tell the other 199 people that, if they follow you and work hard and are honourable and as self-sufficient as possible in all ways, they will receive respect and protection from the entire tribe and its leadership; yet, if idleness and greed and extreme pleasure to the detriment of others is sought, the respect and protection and love will all be withdrawn.

Some may choose the liberal pacifist leader because he or she sounds 'nice' and 'kind' and 'understanding'; yet this individual is of course not a leader and certainly not a protector, owing to their very first acts imperilling the future survival of the tribe.

The first course of action is establishing rules and boundaries; then the strengths and talents and abilities of the survivors would individually need to be established to determine what the leader was capable of achieving with the tribe. Could this group be mustered to construct a seafaring vessel? Do they have the physical and intellectual ability and humility and work ethic to achieve that feat? Are some of the survivors anarchists, nihilists, or antisocial career criminals? This is vitally important information because without knowing who the fellow survivors are, without knowing what tools you are working with, what threats are among you and what anti-threats (police officers/soldiers/guards/vigilantes) are among the group, it will be impossible to lead the tribe and micro nation effectively.

The woke liberal leader-to-be will care not about vital information whilst merely telling folk to 'do their best' when they are politely requested to help collect firewood or coconuts.

Some may argue that 'it's different' in the real world, that liberalism in cities is fine, perfectly acceptable, due to the safety nets of credit and welfare and high taxes and socialised medicine and the service industry and poverty and inequality serving to motivate the most desperate folk at the bottom to serve, to feed, to protect and assist those who vote for liberals. Yet, the more liberal the city becomes the more the city comes to look like San Francisco, which holds many inglorious records at time of writing, including being the 'smash and grab' capital of the world, with few San Franciscans untouched by their vehicles being broken into at least once or twice in their lives.

Balance is needed. Empathy and love are of course important, but so is a strong fist when civilisation and civility and peace and harmony and our children are threatened by those who add nothing but take everything.

Just two or three fentanyl users or heroin users on that island with the survivors would have led to the destruction of the tribe under liberal leadership, whereas under unwoke, illiberal leadership, the heroin and fentanyl addicts on the island would get clean and sober within the first week. No tolerance, no clean needles, just a simple choice: 'Rejoin society, work damn hard—or start swimming!'

Chapter Thirty-Two—How Voluntary Taxation Will Prevent Fascism from Rising Again in the West

'And I'd do it again, too. There's no chance in keeping me alive or anything, because I'd kill again. I have hate crawling through my system.'
—Aileen Wuornos, who murdered at least seven people. She pleaded guilty to many of the offences and admitted she had killed for profit and not in self-defence.

(This chapter originally appeared in the book *Make America United Again: The Trump-Harris Co-Presidency 2024 – 2028*)

You can easily and swiftly take the passion and sentiment out of so many political disagreements and arguments (whilst guarding against fascism and authoritarianism rising) by simply introducing a tweak to the tax system—via implementing the pinnacle of democratic evolution: Voluntary Taxation, also known as Opt-In Taxation.

Democrat voters in the USA can, via the use of this innovative tax system, opt in to pay additional tax to fund every cause they support, be it abortion, be it paying for refugees to be housed; whatever the individual values the most, he or she will be empowered to be able to get involved and know exactly where the tax dollars are being spent.

Republican voters in the USA will have the same ability, as will independents and libertarians, with only those in support of walls paying for walls and only those who are in favour of socialised medicine paying to fund socialised medicine for instance. This system will end internal division and angst immediately as most anger and hate comes from a sense of powerlessness and poverty.

If Opt-In Taxation was implemented under a Harris-Trump Co-Presidency it would counter any and all Democrat complaints about issues such as welfare, immigration, prisons/jails, crime and punishment and so much else as, when Harris tells Trump, 'I want more money spent on the care of illegal immigrants,' Trump replies with, 'Let folk decide individually if they want to pay more tax to fund the care, accommodation, healthcare, education, utilities and feeding of tens of millions of illegal immigrants. If it's what they want, they will choose to opt in so they can pay more tax, won't they?'

Voluntary Taxation, or Opt-In Taxation, resolves seemingly contentious and deadlocked issues immediately via two means, either defunding the programme/government department completely and offering all citizens the ability to immediately opt in to pay more tax individually or as businesses or corporations (Opt-In applies to all, rich and poor, individuals and businesses alike) or via a people's vote, a referendum, on the individual issues if the 'other side' do not wish for the people to choose where their tax dollars are spent. He or she who is staunchly against referendums needs to be removed from power in democratic nations via the ballot box as that person desires minority rule and is thus an enemy of the people.

The vanity projects of the left (as the right would call them) would only be paid for by liberals, Democrats, and left-leaning internationalists and anti-borders folk in general who would be required to send an SMS, make a phone call, fill out a form online or in person in order to request that they pay more tax for these government departments or projects and for the principles and ideology of the privileged elite few to be brought to life via the aid of billions being paid in tax. Those who are opposed to the wants of a minority (and who do not suffer from privileged or liberal guilt and who cannot afford to pay a cent more in taxation) should of course not be forced to pay for these projects/social engineering.

If you do not contact the government, your tax bill will noticeably reduce, whilst those who desire to share the fruits of their labours with others (think foreign aid/aid for illegal immigrants/legal aid) would be the only ones paying to sustain such things. Their tax rate would keep rising for so long as they wished to maintain their principled, virtuous stance and cultish need to self-abnegate.

The recently published guide to this democratic tax system, which reduces friction, ill feeling and tribalism between citizens and classes, will benefit all hardworking Americans and individual parties and will be of great benefit to the proposed union of Democrats and Republicans.

The Co-Presidency adopting Opt-In Taxation would mean the people are united together but able to separately choose whether or not they choose to individually fund the wants of the few, with it being inconceivable for the unwoke, for libertarians or patriots to ever pay to fund progressive, liberal, anti-patriotic projects and causes, just as pacifist liberals might want to opt out of having to fund border walls or the manufacturing of more American flags. It works both ways.

If you support abortion, you may wish to pay more in tax to increase abortions, but if you do not support even a single abortion, you should not be expected to pay for abortion—for many this is beyond an ethical issue, it is a religious/spiritual issue.

If the Republicans are the majority party, Democrats may wish to opt out of certain aspects of their agenda and vice versa.

***

On the modern neo-liberal, progressive, ever more woke 'nice guy' left (the words woke and liberal are both code for high functioning or "superior", it should be known) there exist collective shared beliefs that are top down from the most privileged thought leaders, with self-abnegation, masochism and a globalist, borderless world outlook at their core. Their decisions are driven by guilt. Whilst on the Republican, conservative, nationalist right there are similar collected beliefs. Like their counterparts on the left, they are forced into a groupthink collective mindset, which is hard to deviate from, with a fear of moving towards the centre or ever admitting that, for instance, guns in the hands of the mentally ill is a bad thing.

The fear of both tribal groups, who have tethered their hearts and psyches to a particular team, which compels them to remain staunchly loyal and tribal (in public at least), primarily derives from a desire to maintain power or increase power, and in the modern era, money = power.

With this in mind, to ensure a swift end to groupthink and to ensure we never again witness a reprisal of the NSDAP phenomenon, all we need do is empower every single citizen concurrently by introducing voluntary taxation as, at its heart, it is a means to end hate, end inter-human violence and conflict, end political and racial extremism and ensure that the psychopaths and nihilists and anarchists in our midst can never again lead good men astray resulting in certain genocides down the road, avoidable genocides.

Once the folk on the right who refuse to budge an inch on certain issues realise that they no longer have to pay extra taxes upon the occasion of the left winning an electoral victory, however narrow, by virtue of voluntary taxation their anger, hate, vitriol and prejudice will all DISAPPEAR, why?

Because money is power and when the left force right-wingers to pay more tax in order to fund their self-abnegating and masochism and guilt and 'nice guy' driven benevolent polices and ideals, the right become far-right.

Right-wingers are fine with migrants moving to left-wingers' neighbourhoods; they are happy for multiculturalism to find Martha's Vineyard or Mayfair or any other elite enclaves.

***

Voluntary taxation would end all friction in regards to immigration, refugees, foreign aid, charity, abortion, the death penalty, crime and punishment, prisons and much else.

When you do not have to pay for the things you absolutely hate with all of your heart and being, you become instantly far friendlier to the other voter who does want to fund these things, who will still be able to but will now have to pay for these things on their own.

'I hate abortion!'

'But you don't have to pay for abortion anymore. Only your political opposites and rivals are paying for abortions now, which is impoverishing them.'

'I feel happier now.'

'I hate having to pay a fortune, an absolute fortune for paedophiles to be kept alive for twenty years in prison after killing one or multiple children! And I hate having to pay for their care and housing and healthcare upon release also!'

'But you no longer have to pay to keep them in prison. Only your political opposites and rivals are paying to keep violent rapists, paedophiles, killers, terrorists and traitors in prison now; only they are being financially harmed due to them being opposed to capital punishment for serious crimes against the people and state.'

'I feel a lot happier now … and I am wealthier also due to Opt-In Taxation. Let the tolerant ones alone pay to keep such folk alive and let them be rehoused only in areas where the majority opt in to fund prisons and the life-extension of killers and terrorists and rapists and enemies of the people.'

***

Rather than be miserable and extremely tribal and zealous, it is better to only pay for what you want. This will create hitherto unimagined peace and harmony and, most importantly, equality and a resurgence of people power and democracy.

It is very easy to insist one and all should pay to fund the same causes as yourself when your bank balance is huge; yet, the worker is most likely the victim of demographic change, of crime, of recidivism, of mass immigration, rising rents and lowering wages, of imported drugs, of gangs, of corrupt public officials or abusive members of the clergy. The worker, the humble worker, is most often the victim in real life, in the real world, meaning he feels doubly hurt and victimised when he witnesses taxes increasing.

An ugly inequality is then created and an immoral state is birthed as the victims of most rape and murder and violent crime and home invasions and antisocial neighbours and deprivation and all else that is bad in society are then expected to pay to house their abusers in luxury in prison and thereafter to pay to house them once again within their community—as criminals are rarely rehabilitated in privileged liberal enclaves.

This is why we need Voluntary Taxation, to prevent oppressed underclasses from seeking desperate escapism and solace in the welcoming arms of the far right or the far left.

Chapter Thirty-Three—The People's Protection Contract

"How about this for a headline for tomorrow's paper? French fries."

—James French prior to his execution. He murdered a driver who picked him up when French was hitchhiking. Given a life sentence for killing the Good Samaritan, French decided that he no longer wished to live once imprisoned, but due to the fact that he didn't wish to kill himself he instead violently killed his cellmate as a means to compel the state to execute him.

(This chapter originally appeared in the book *Make America United Again: The Trump-Harris Co-Presidency 2024 – 2028*)

CORRUPTION, *noun* [Latin]

The act of corrupting, or state of being corrupt or putrid; <u>the destruction of the natural form of bodies, by the separation of the component parts, or by disorganization</u>, in the process of putrefaction.

I've underlined the pertinent meaning in the sense of political, union and religious corruption committed by those who abuse their position of privilege, trust and power.

A body cannot long survive when its arms or legs become damaged, and are politicians not our arms, are priests and union officials not our legs?

When these components of the body succumb to corruption, they become decayed and worthless, causing a relentless rot, a festering disease that in the shortest imaginable time shall cause the absolute destruction of the body, leaving behind nothing but a worthless and irredeemable corpse.

But there is another way.

If the body received an inoculation against the spread of corruption, if a vaccine existed and could be administered in time before riots and revolutions became necessary, before we blindly followed the corrupt into another world war, then the body could be saved. The People's Protection Contract is the vaccine.

***

The People's Protection Contract (PPC) ensures the public are protected from the actions of corrupt, treasonous, and compromised (blackmailed) public servants who use their temporary positions of trust and responsibility and power to illegally enrich themselves, damage the nation/people, provide benefits to competitor nations or foreign corporations and businesses as well as ensuring against nepotism, bribe-taking and corruption locally and nationally at the political level.

This proposed document, just one page in length, is a promise to the people from he or she who voluntarily signs it, with the wording and content likely varying from nation to nation. Those who choose to write down such a contract and sign it will make that fact known to one and all, certainly guaranteeing them landslide victories in nations stung and laid low by corruption and bribery and similar scandals involving political corruption, nepotism, cover-ups and sleaze.

The need for such a contract, separate from one's party affiliation, separate from party manifesto/platform, is great in 2024 as a means to restore public confidence in institutions and in the democratic representative process as so many have become hit by apathy and malaise. So many have surrendered to cynicism after witnessing folk on both sides of the aisle lying to their faces, engaging in obvious corruption and then leaving office multimillionaires every single time without fail. This can only last for so long before the entire system collapses, self-implodes.

Currently, it is hard to remove a senator, MP, prime minister, president, congressman or woman, it is damn hard, because they and their colleagues decide the rules and laws, which often include 'parliamentary privilege' or 'parliamentary immunity' with certain nations, such as the US, for instance, even permitting paid public servants the ability to refuse to answer questions due to being protected by amendments and constitutions.

The PPC changes all of this because the PPC is all about honour.

If a representative signs this contract, which will ensure he/she is elected, and they later are found to be corrupt, there will be no need to wait until that person has completed their term in order to remove them from power as the clause in every such contract to 'agree to immediately leave office' if they ever refuse to answer questions or if they ever attempt to hide behind parliamentary privilege/immunity will ensure that either:

The politician will refrain from engaging in any acts of treason, fifth columnism, nepotism, corruption or abuse of power in any way, shape or form or,

The politician will have to fall on their sword the moment they are discovered to have abused their position of power, authority, responsibility and trust. Most politicians will not write into such a contract that they will literally fall on their swords if they fail the people; few will sign a document stating they will request execution, with most, however, happily signing that they will immediately retire, even if only one month into a four-year elected term.

The PPC is a list of pledges, in effect, which infuse a much needed powerful means to hold public servants accountable whilst keeping them honest and honourable and committed to doing the best possible job— every soul who runs for election, of every kind, should happily desire to sign a PPC document, with only those intent on theft and deception and harming the community/nation refusing to sign such a pro-democracy and pro-people-power contract.

Confidence and Trust

The PPC restores trust and multiplies confidence in the political system, ensuring against a one-party state or fascism, ensuring that democracy survives as more folk than ever from all walks of life begin voting, perhaps many for the first time in their lives, as the PPC is an apathy destroyer and a huge motivator.

Our police officers are, for the most part, well thought of. They do a dangerous job, their lives are always at risk on an hourly basis; yet these unsung heroes are (in many democracies in 2024) compelled against their will to wear body cameras. This change has increased public trust in the police and minimised accusations of corruption and foul play, and if it is the case that citizens as well as police chiefs and politicians all agree that surveillance of one type of public servant (police officers) via audio and video recording hardware has decreased corruption whilst super-charging public confidence, it stands to reason that politicians and civil servants in general should similarly wear such technology, or at least have audio/video recording facilities placed within their homes and offices. Those who sign a PPC stating they would happily be monitored by any and all means are true public servants with nothing to hide, rather than being potentially huge security risks, fifth columnists or merely just corrupt and desiring to hide their corruption.

The contract would include guarantees that would put the minds of all at ease as to the true nature of individual politicians, their parties and the political system as a whole—with some guarantees by those who sign these documents immediately ending paranoia, fear and conspiracy theorism, whilst other items within the signed document would keep organised crime out of politics and take away the power that foreign states/competitor nations are currently able to exert over those who have expensive addictions/tastes.

Below is a sample People's Protection Contract form. Once all politicians routinely, habitually sign such documents, every democracy shall be perfect, healthy, corruption-free and solvent.

***

I am not a member of a secret society. I will never join or work on behalf of a secret society. I do not represent a business, corporation or a foreign state, nor will I ever represent the interests of anyone other than native citizens under pain of death/forfeiture of all assets, loss of employment, loss of pension, loss of citizenship and loss of all rights and freedoms.

I do not accept bribes and I will never accept bribes in the future.

I am not being blackmailed or controlled by any criminal organisation at home or abroad, nor will I ever consent to be. I will report any attempts to control, coerce or bribe or threaten me immediately to the people. If I observe crime or corruption or political interference in any fashion I will report it to the people, all of the people, immediately.

I am not part of a conspiracy, I am not a fifth-columnist, I am not compromised or owned in any way. I have free will. I will serve the people to the very best of my ability or happily be removed from my position of trust and responsibility if I fail the people.

I swear, under pain of death, that I will never lie to the people.

I agree to leave office immediately if found guilty of any crimes or misconduct.

I have not been compromised by any individual or business, corporation or foreign state. I am not being and cannot be blackmailed; any attempts to blackmail or control me will be immediately reported to the people—immediately.

I do not work for any business, corporation, individual or foreign state. I am an individual who owes their loyalty solely to the people, all of the people, whom I will serve to the very best of my ability.

I agree to any type of surveillance; my freedoms and privacy are forfeit for so long as I am a public servant. I consent to the use of body cams, video and audio surveillance as well as random drug/alcohol tests. I will be fully transparent and fully accountable.

I sign this contract knowing full well that if I ever take a bribe, engage in nepotism or corruption, collude with corporations or foreign governments or share state secrets or classified information with competitor nations or those who will pass such information to competitor nations, my career, possessions, pension, reputation and citizenship and rights and freedoms are forfeit/my life is forfeit.

Signed ………………………….. Date …………..

Is this a drastic and revolutionary step? Yes. But would you sign this document? Yes, without a thought, if you are a good patriot and honest man or woman, which is why we need measures such as these in all good democracies, to strangle corruption and crime dead, immediately.

These three entities, secret societies, corporations and external enemies, will be the only ones against American unity because unity strengthens, which is why the wise Americans who built the Lincoln monument depicted something on his mighty eternal throne that many Americans will find curious upon seeing it for the first time—many sticks bound together, forming collectively a single powerful entity, symbolising an unbreakable union; because you are stronger, because you are unbreakable when you are united.

Incentivising Honour, Honesty and Responsibility

There is a general election; the people need to choose 500 representatives to represent them (think MPs/senators). The population is, for instance, ten million.

Initially 25,000 men and women step forward, wishing to be representatives.

This figure soon decreases as individual parties choose their preferred candidate—the one who they believe stands the greatest chance of winning and who is most loyal to the party and its leadership.

Eventually, the number of prospective representatives decreases to only 5,000, with 4,500 representing the various established parties and the remaining 500 standing as independents.

The 4,500 representatives linked to parties will likely refuse to sign any declaration or contract that commits them to being honourable and non-treasonous—their party will almost certainly tell them not to agree to anything.

The remaining 500 independent representatives, however, will not rule out signing such a declaration and fully committing themselves to being the representative the people deserve.

On election night, if all 4,500 party-affiliated representatives refused to sign the People's Protection Contract (which means they refuse to be held accountable for their criminality, bribe-taking and stealing money from the people, which means they are not responsible or trustworthy representatives) but the 500 independent candidates enthusiastically, loudly and confidently signed the declaration, what will the new Senate or Parliament or Congress look like? How would you vote?

Only independent representatives will be elected to office so long as the people are not totally lost to co-dependence and masochism. Every party will cease to be—because to be an enemy of those who are fighting a war against corruption and treason (those who sign the declaration) is to reveal your true character, a character that has been bastardised due to immersion in corruption, sleaze, shadowy deals, handshakes in hotel rooms and countless suitcases full of cash, be it from foreign nations or from the people's treasury.

Any complaint about 'having to face justice' for being treasonous will be laughed at by the people, who will have no sympathy for those who have continually hoodwinked and betrayed them. The people will say, 'If you can't do the job honestly, go. Just go, and then you won't need to worry about justice or responsibility—move into the private sector, immediately.'

The politician who signs a PPC, which states, 'I will agree to a twenty-year prison sentence (which should be the mandatory minimum sentence, funded solely by the acquisition of all property and possessions seized from the offender) if I ever take a bribe, fail to report corruption around me or if I ever steal money from the people,' will be re-elected again and again and again.

If he/she is ever found guilty of the transgressions mentioned above, it will be as though the representative has chosen to imprison themselves or, in the case of those brave enough to sign the Voluntary Execution Declaration, it will be as though the representative has committed suicide because it must be seen as suicidal to dare to hurt the people by being corrupt. Such acts will not be repeated moving forward because no man is forced to represent his people and no man is forced to betray his people.

Why don't I like the Third Reich? Because all the unions except one were banned and the news and media were controlled by the party, by one party. Corruption, greed and abuse of power reigned supreme as a result, with the brown-shirt liberators outdoing their forebears (just as was the case following the Russian revolution) in terms of control, persecution, micromanaging the people and owning them mind, body and soul.

The Third Reich wasn't the triumph of the will; it was the failure of scared voters, of ordinary citizens to demand good order, honourable representatives and a corruption-free-nation. Hitler's achievements and successes were hollow because he didn't trust the people to be anything more than the builders of his new empire, tools to be used, which he dominated and controlled far too much, spreading fear and Stockholm syndrome near and far, with many convinced that they were actually living worthwhile, valuable full lives despite democracy and freedom being suddenly suspended and every twentieth man being forced to wear an ominous and foreboding yellow star on his coat.

The triumph of the will occurs on the day when every people's representative insists on signing a blood contract with the people they represent, which guarantees peace, stability, good order and honest leadership.

If the people ever choose to vote for the man who refuses to sign a PPC when many others have willingly signed such a pro-democracy, pro-honesty, pro-transparency and pro-people-power guarantee that corruption will die, they will know what awaits them as they sacrifice freedom and solvency and pride and democracy in favour of party affiliation and temporary and extremely fleeting self-service.

Once it is widely known that prospective candidates can, if they so choose, sign a document (a PPC) and take it along with them when campaigning or canvassing, handing out copies even to folk, savvy voters will ask candidates from their own party and competing parties whether or not they have signed a People's Protection Contract yet, to which the reply will invariably (at first at least) be 'No.'

Yet, once voters inform them about the other candidates signing such documents, such a list of guaranteed pledges that restore balance and sanity and honesty in the political system and institutions, he who says 'No,' will soon reply instead, 'Not yet, but I will.'

If you are a candidate for any political office and tell folk (whose vote you need to be elected) the following and they vote for you, they will be voting for corruption and mismanagement and disorder, surrender, crime, weakness and apathy and failure.

'I will never, never ever sign a contract in front of the people that guarantees I cannot be corrupt, treasonous or nepotistic due to such a contract leading to me being exiled, stripped of rights/citizenship, sent to prison (for life), losing all my assets or agreeing to voluntary execution if I commit crimes against the people and nation.'

Honest men, honest women are already drafting their own versions of the People's Protection Contract for the next elections in their respective homelands, knowing it will be a great talking point when attempting to secure votes and support as they tell the people they meet, 'The other candidates will never sign such a contract, which is why they need to be voted out, defunded and retired.'

I will always vote for the candidate who signs a PPC, I care not what his party affiliation is, I care not to see them kissing babies or smiling or waving to crowds, I care not how nice the candidate's dress or suit is; all that matters is honesty, accountability, responsibility and integrity. All else is secondary because a smile does not guarantee a corruption-free political term; nice hair, nice makeup, nice speeches do not guarantee a corruption-free political term, but the People's Protection Contract does as it kills corruption, just as it terminates political failure and treason and nullifies fifth columnism whilst simultaneously guarding against authoritarianism and fascism.

***

Voluntary Execution

When men and women become unnaturally powerful due to others paying them to represent the people/nation (because they promised to be kind and good servants), the very last thing on their mind is their own demise. The opposite is true; they wish to ascend and keep ascending. It's all that matters to many politicians in life, the temporary acquisition of wealth and power to the detriment of the people: Saboteurs of civilisation.

So, many would find it odd that such obsessive and self-loving/self-serving individuals (to accept bribes, to steal from pensioners you cannot be a typical and healthy-minded individual) would ever consent to such a thing as a 'Voluntary Execution' upon the occasion of them accepting bribes or stealing money from the people, being treasonous and criminal.

Yet, surely representatives or candidates desiring to be representatives who are driven by 'duty' and guiding principles and beliefs would have absolutely no problem is signing a Voluntary Execution contract with the people, because such a person would never breach such a contract, would they? Because,

1/ They don't want to die and

2/ They would never accept bribes, abuse their power or steal from the people.

Meaning, those who do not choose to voluntarily sign a PPC which includes a voluntary execution clause are certifiably corrupt and intent on stealing, taking bribes, being nepotistic, selling out the people/nation and betraying the people at every turn to the benefit of corporations or competitor nations, whereas, those who sign a PPC which includes a voluntary execution clause are certifiably honest, trustworthy, law-abiding and dutiful servants of the majority will, rather than ceasers-to-be.

Voluntary execution means they who sign such a PPC agree to fall on their sword, immediately go into exile, or agree to be executed by the state, a suicide in effect, due to them knowing the consequences of their actions, if caught breaking laws and trust.

Chapter Thirty-Four—Death for Treason

'I remember there was actually a sexual thrill ... you hear that little pop and pull their heads off and hold their heads up by the hair. Whipping their heads off, their body sitting there. That'd get me off.'

—Edmund Kemper, who killed eight people. As a teenager he killed his grandparents to 'see what it felt like.' He coerced his sisters into playing a game he called 'gas chamber', in which he had them blindfold him and lead him to a chair, where he pretended to writhe in agony until he "died".

(This chapter originally appeared in the book *Make America United Again: The Trump-Harris Co-Presidency 2024 – 2028*)

Too much state power is a bad thing and giving the state the power to execute a person, even if that person is the worst human being imaginable (a corrupt people's representative), can be advantageous when the people collectively hold all representatives (from unions, political parties and organised religions) accountable at all times; yet, the moment people look away, even if just for a moment, those same politicians and representatives who yesterday were exposed and punished for their crimes now have the 'power of God'—because they have the ability to legally kill their rivals, you, the people.

It is for this reason that one must tread carefully so as not to make the 'corrupt beast' more powerful. This beast will be tamed and rehabilitated rather than killed because if we wish to enjoy the gifts that a free and honourable world will grant us, we need to be both honourable and loving in how we discipline and educate those who transgress against the people they are sworn to protect and represent.

It is not necessary to threaten execution for treason; rather, it should be for individual politicians (and prospective representatives in general) to choose for themselves whether or not they will tell potential voters (whilst canvassing/campaigning) either:

'I never want treasonous and/or corrupt politicians to be executed, even if they are the direct cause of thousands of our pensioners freezing to death in winter or the cause of wars or national bankruptcy.'

Or

'I support the death penalty for treason, which includes accepting bribes or stealing money from the people. I am willing to be executed if I commit treason.'

Which statement do you think the voter wishes to hear, the first or the second?

Which statement do you think the prospective politician will be forced to make if all of the people are united in a 'war against corruption and treason'?

Some voters, some very masochistic voters, might reply, 'Oh no, you shouldn't have to be punished just for stealing a few million dollars/pounds/euros; shouldn't you just do some probation, community service or something similar, or pay a fine?'

Such people, thankfully, are a tiny minority of the electorate—who are the chief enablers of corruption and treason and societal devolution.

The majority desire decisive action, the majority desire responsibility and accountability. If a man tries to rob me, carjack me, or invade my home, one of us will die. I am not the only one who feels this way; I am not the only one who is willing to die for freedom and liberty at the drop of a hat.

The people as a whole feel the same way, they will kill and die to defend their children and loved ones—which is why corruption and treason within nations and unions leaves a bad taste in the mouth in 2024, because such acts are arrogant opportunism but hidden and stealthy opportunism, cowardly opportunism.

Have no sympathy for such individuals, they have removed themselves from the community, the corrupt are easily banish-worthy; yet, who would wish to inflict such inglorious fellows on our neighbouring countries?

The corrupt few (the treasonous few) remain arrogant and defiant as they continue to plunder the fruits of the people's labour guessing that they (the people) will never be smart enough to understand what corruption is, what constitutes a bribe, what constitutes a gift and just what it is, exactly, that their representatives do for them—other than taxing them and stealing from them after taxing them.

Corrupt representatives rely on voter ignorance and voter apathy—their two best friends.

It is for this reason that every man and woman needs to involve themselves as fully as possible in politics or unions (whatever is relevant in their case, in terms of corruption and abuse of power).

It doesn't matter if you find yourself on the left or the right, the centre or the far left or the far right—all that matters is you are getting involved, proving that you care and have not surrendered to apathy and nihilism, because if no one stands up to a bully, the bully begins to believe that his behaviour is normal.

Whatever your belief system or partisan view, you certainly share common goals with every voter and activist who supports other parties, even those who are the main competitors of yours. Do Republican and Democrat voters in the USA both desire good order, peace and civilisation? Yes. Do Labour, Conservative and Liberal Democrat voters in the UK desire good order, peace and civilisation? Yes.

We are the same.

Our differences are tiny, they are exaggerated.

What we have in common are our shared purpose, our shared passion for life, our refusal to be victims of crime and corruption, and our insistence that our employees/public servants (union officials, police officers, politicians, priests, etc.) do a great job without stealing from us or abusing the power we temporarily grant them.

We are the same.

Chapter Thirty-Five—Restructuring of Welfare, Housing and Healthcare Systems

"Freedom, freedom at last! It's been a good one!"
—John W. Rook, who kidnapped and raped a hospital nurse before running her body over with his car. These were his last words before his execution.

(This chapter originally appeared in the book Ending the Migrant Crisis in Europe: Preventing Class Wars, Race Wars and the Destruction of the EU)

As has been evidenced convincingly elsewhere within this work, the vast majority of migrants and refugees entering Europe choose to gravitate towards those nations with the most generous welfare/benefit systems. Those refugees who have made it to France, a great and free and generous nation, often choose to risk their lives by crossing the treacherous English Channel in small dinghies. This proves that they are not refugees but opportunists. They are not in danger in France; rather, they are willingly putting themselves in danger by risking drowning in order to make it to the UK mainland where they will scream, 'Asylum, asylum! Please give me a British passport and a house and money.'

This is a legacy of empire, with many economic migrants who pose as refugees (because they wish to be kept for life) wrongly believing that Britain still 'rules the waves'. These days, Britain is massively overpopulated and a shadow of her former imperialist self; however, other than being drawn to Britain's 'power', fake refugees come for welfare, for housing, for healthcare and it will all be free in perpetuity, why? Because of the struggles and sacrifices of the working class and unions in the past. A lot of marches, a lot of strikes, and a lot of hard work secured social benefits and welfare and state housing and education for the poor. These things were not benevolent gifts from the elites or middle class; no, these things took immense struggle and upheaval.

The obvious fact is if Britain stated tomorrow that all welfare payments, all social benefits and pensions and free healthcare and free stuff full stop were all going to end, no more money for anyone unless they worked hard (which seems logical and fair) there would no longer be economic migrants, criminals and opportunists posing as refugees crossing the Channel, endangering their own lives as well as the lives of French and British coastguards. As a result, the number of migrants present in France would drop massively overnight, reducing the burden on that already overburdened caring and compassionate country.

Imagine that Britain no longer gave away anything for free to her own citizens or foreigners, why would a single migrant and refugee choose to take the additional trip across the ocean rather than settling in Germany or Italy or Romania or Poland? Why would any of these individuals want to come to Britain if there was no free house for them, no free healthcare for them, no pension for them, no free welfare payments every week, no free food for them, no free furniture for them, no free utilities for them, no free gas, no free water, no free electricity for them, no free smartphone and phone contract for them, no free legal assistance for them, and no free translation services for them all paid for by the hardworking and overburdened British worker?

The easiest way to end the problem of fake refugees as well as mass immigration is to stop giving everything away for free. This is madness, we cannot afford this. Taxes should reduce every year as we socially and intellectually evolve and as we reduce corruption, overcome crime and create utopias throughout the world. Tax should never rise, yet that is what happens every year, not including the stealth taxes such as rising rents and stagnation of wages at a time of high inflation due to the missteps of our national representatives....

Instead of saying to the poor of the world, 'Come to France, everything is free here,' or, 'Come to Britain, everything is free here,' one should say, 'Come here if you have something to contribute. We are willing to protect you but only if you are willing to protect us in return and become loyal to our nation, to sever old allegiances, to know and love our language and culture before you reach our shores, only if you integrate rather than self-segregate and self-ghettoise, only if you agree to pay back every single penny or cent loaned to you via the 'Welfare Loan System'. If an alleged refugee arrives with nothing, it will perhaps cost €50,000 to pay for his integration, accommodation, new clothes and furniture, healthcare, dental care and food for the first twelve to twenty-four months. This sum must be paid back; the generosity part is that this is an interest-free loan.

Those migrants/refugees who do not like this concept can apply for asylum elsewhere; they can drain someone else's treasury. The current situation is disgraceful and the cause of widespread racism and abject hatred of refugees, which sounds bizarre but is a reality because the soft and liberal welfare and benefits systems of the West treat foreigners with kid gloves, not wishing to appear racist in any way, because that is career suicide in this politically correct age. Clearly the combination of softness, liberalism and political correctness is not solving any problems but rather is the cause of problems multiplying for everyone.

There have been multiple cases of fake refugees, criminals posing as refugees and terrorists posing as refugees, including, for instance the cases of Khairi Saadallah, Emad al-Swealmeen and many others also who were granted asylum by Britain only to commit serious and deadly terror attacks on British soil afterwards.

The first step to deterring them would be to declare, 'There is no money left, nothing is free here anymore. If we give you money, you will be paying it back when you begin working.' Those who consent to such a reasonable and sensible demand will be deemed by all citizens to be genuine, creating a better atmosphere for all, including the migrants themselves, due to racial tensions and racism reducing overnight.

What do natives everywhere always complain about? Migrants/refugees 'living on welfare'. If it is no longer possible for migrants or natives, then complaints will end and all can focus on their own lives, getting their own houses in order and collectively making their nations into strong and supporting vessels that will carry the people who dwell within into the next millennium.

The Welfare Loan System should also apply to an eighteen-year-old native who claims he can't find work or a fifty-year-old native who claims the same thing, not only to ensure equality between all citizens (native and non-native alike, native born and foreign born, indigenous and refugee alike), meaning that foreigners are being treated just the same as natives, no better, no worse, but also, insisting that jobseekers' benefit/unemployment welfare payments and state funding of rent must always be repaid as soon as possible will have numerous glorious benefits for all nations wise enough to enact these revolutionary changes.

A fourteen-year-old young woman in England or France or Germany today knows that it doesn't matter all that much if she falls pregnant because the state will give her free money, free nappies (diapers), free accommodation, free healthcare, free, free, free, free—yet after this proposed change, she will know that these things are no longer free but rather temporary loans. When the same fourteen-year-old realises that her parents and family will be expected to repay this loan until she becomes an adult when that responsibility shall transfer to her, she will tell her boyfriend, 'When we are adults with work, a roof over our heads and stability, we can have sex. Being irresponsible and out of control now will doom both of our futures. I am not willing to get into so much debt; I haven't even lived yet....'

The Welfare Loan System will:

• End malaise and apathy and smash the depression and pessimism within every native in receipt of these welfare loans due to them suddenly being motivated, for perhaps the first time in their lives, to rise. Where previously there was no pressure to swiftly find work in order to survive, now the longer they choose to stagnate and avoid duty and responsibility the greater the size of their loan becomes.

- End the practice of living beyond one's own means.

- Create a new self-sufficient trend everywhere and cottage industries and self-employment, due to many seeking to escape dependency upon the state eternally (because they soon get bored of paying back the loans given to them for healthcare, dental care, housing payments and free food), which will result in thousands of new micro farms everywhere and hundreds of thousands of new small businesses. Entirely new industries will spring up almost overnight as every man and every woman suddenly stands taller and prouder, now physically and psychologically stronger as obesity and depression and addiction become things of the past, as fast food and self-harm are rejected as all seek a more natural and healthy existence, as credit and debt disappear due to all learning the value of living within one's own means.

- Reduce crime everywhere due to the sudden huge surge in profound self-respect and self-determination achieved via no longer 'giving people free stuff'. The man who yesterday looked the other way when drugs were being sold outside his child's school because of the free house and free food and free healthcare and free bus travel the state gave him will suddenly, in an awesome manner, feel compelled to keep his community and streets clean of any and all crime and criminals, whom he will talk to, whom he will try to reach, but whom he will not allow to terrorise his community a moment longer. When the free money ends, the bribe to be servile ends, so do collective apathy and dereliction of duty. Men everywhere will rise as criminals everywhere hurriedly reform.

- Cause a new love of state, of community, of the system and culture and society to flourish because no one respects the man who gives you free money whenever you ask him to, but everyone respects the man who says, 'I will give you money after you have first completed a useful or worthwhile task.' It is not love to give a man free things because it creates dependency and weakness in his heart, he comes to hate himself and then you, but if you give him work, or, better still, if you do everything possible to encourage him to become self-employed or self-sufficient (more must be done in this area, much more) then he will not only love himself after working for his reward, he will love you also, for not patronising him and for treating him like an equal rather than a ward or a lesser individual.

I would strongly recommend it being a prerequisite to qualify for any welfare loan payments of any kind to be a sober non-smoker with good physical health.

If an individual wants me to give them a loan (what the envisioned welfare/benefit payments would amount to) wouldn't I be a fool for handing over a single penny if the applicant was smoking expensive cigarettes, drinking alcohol, which is in equal parts expensive and demotivating (alcohol is a proven depressant), and morbidly obese?

If two applicants asked me to provide them with a loan, one was a healthy living, fit and self-disciplined man who wasn't killing himself with cigarettes or alcohol or drugs or similar self-harming behaviours and the other was the complete opposite, whom would I offer the loan to if I had to choose between the two men?

The 'nice guy' in me would feel inclined to help the man who seemed more desperate, who was destroying himself via his numerous addictions and a toxic lifestyle, clearly depressed, clearly long before having chosen to give up. But that would penalise the other man who made his bed at 7:30 a.m. even when he was out of work, who then ran five miles and completed several sets of push-ups and sit-ups before having a cold shower. This other man, this Spartan, this useful citizen, this patriot would deserve my full attention and the loan, whereas the other man should be starved of funds until his unnecessary and harmful addictions and habits fell away from him as he became physically and psychologically fit and healthy, for perhaps the first time in his life—boot camp/military service without the need for these troubled souls to be sent away anywhere. It is far better to trust people (especially men) to improve themselves alone, gradually, in order to build in them the type of character that will attract the best type of friends to them, the type of character that will attract the best mates to them and the type of character that will attract the best employers to them.

Such a system cannot be implemented overnight. Warnings would have to be given far in advance of the change in order to ensure that those who smoke, drink, have terrible diets and lead depressingly sedentary, unnatural lives, primarily in front of the television or in pubs or sports stadiums, would be able to adapt to the new universally beneficial order with the least amount of trauma and shock caused to them.

The interesting benefit of requiring those you help to be fit and healthy and non-smoking, self-disciplined and self-motivating non-drug users and non-alcoholics is that the education system and the media would naturally come to champion this cause as there are no downsides; everyone wins. Only apathy, pessimism, cynicism, depression, obesity and liver disease and cancer die! Let these things die!

The irony of insisting that a citizen could only qualify for state assistance if he was in optimum fighting fit health is that the moment he found himself out of work and standing in the queue outside the government welfare office where he would apply for a temporary welfare loan he would look himself up and down as he felt fear inside due to being unemployed and embarrassment and shame due to having to beg the state for a loan.

And then he would realise that only the 'old him' needed help from anyone because the fear he was now feeling was an echo from before when he had expensive smoking and drinking and drug habits, when he lived a vain and affected life where he "needed" to spend a fortune on clothes and jewellery and the latest expensive phone, becoming something strangely artificial and certainly not human in the traditional sense.

This citizen, now self-disciplined and exercising complete self-control, in amazing physical and psychological health, would smile before leaving the queue. He would find a pen from his pocket, he would find a piece of cardboard in a bin he walked past, and, whilst continuing to smile from ear to ear, he would write down his CV and abilities as he walked through his local town shouting in a friendly manner to others as he held his sign proudly before him, 'I do not want to burden the state by applying for welfare. My previous employment ended one hour ago, I am ready to continue working immediately. I will do any kind of work; I will be an asset to you.' Within one hour he would find himself again in employment. Within five years he would be a regional manager. Within fifteen years he would own his own business, employing hundreds, and he would have done it all himself!

Man wants to thrive; we need to let him thrive. Survival is not enough. The meaning of life is not for humans to merely survive by subsisting off the state.

Chapter Thirty-Six—The Death of Silicon Valley and US Corporations

"I don't care if I live or die. Go ahead and kill me."
—Jeffrey Dahmer, who raped and killed seventeen men and boys in the 1980s.

In the USA there are numerous large tech, software and social media companies/corporations that routinely make billions in profit each year globally, whose shares can be purchased and sold, which have consistently risen in value these past years as a result of ad revenue. The same is true of many other corporations and big businesses, with the majority of these 'trendy' corporations being left-leaning, liberal and (seemingly) in favour of higher taxes for the people yet consistently desiring to pay as low tax as possible themselves—there are no corporations in the USA in 2024 who desire corporation tax to drastically increase, not a single one.

So how could a well-established monopoly-esque business or corporation like Alphabet/Google or Microsoft, Apple or Facebook be felled? How could the entirety of Silicon Valley and household names such as Facebook and Google and YouTube all suddenly, virtually overnight, go completely bankrupt and disappear? Let me explain; it is really rather easy to achieve, child's play in fact.

These businesses/corporations have shareholders.

If those who own shares all suddenly attempted to sell their shares, the value of the corporations would plummet to nothingness, nothingness.

So the question is what would compel each and every investor in, for instance, Google/YouTube/Facebook/Microsoft to immediately offload each and every share, precipitating a downward spiral for the corporation and a very sudden and shocking demise?

The answer is the enactment of Opt-In Taxation in tandem with Google/YouTube/big tech in general and Silicon Valley as a whole bowing to cancel culture peer pressure from a minority of social justice warriors for them (as a responsible and progressive and liberal and tolerant and caring and compassionate enterprise) to opt in to pay extra in corporate taxes as a means to offset the harm to certain social programs and foreign aid budgets caused by the vast majority of citizens choosing to opt out of funding these things—this would be the beginning of the end, the absolute beginning of the end for any corporation.

Here is an oversimplified series of events that demonstrates the decline and then death of Google/YouTube/Facebook/Silicon Valley in general:

Opt-In Taxation is introduced.

The vast majority choose not to opt in to fund the housing/healthcare of illegal immigrants; the majority choose not to opt in to fund foreign aid; the majority choose not to fund methadone or facilities or care for violent or sexual offenders.

A minority of wokevists and social justice warriors then bully and harass every US corporation, demanding to know if they are choosing to opt in to pay more in tax in order to fund the departments and causes and services and "ideals" that the majority of the citizenry have chosen to defund.

Corporations bow to the pressure. They declare that they will now benevolently be opting in to pay more tax to fund fringe issues, to advantage foreign citizens and to give the minority what they want.

Folk, regular folk, who happen to own Google/YouTube/Facebook/Silicon Valley/telecoms companies shares, perhaps just a few hundred dollars' worth, perhaps a few hundred thousand dollars' worth, all suddenly fear that profits will now go down due to the corporation willingly agreeing to pay more tax.

The investors (a majority of them) will immediately cash in their shares in the corporations that have chosen to opt in, choosing to instead wisely invest their money only in corporations that have publicly stated they will NEVER choose to pay more in taxation than is legally required.

Within a few days, the corporations that have chosen to opt in will no longer exist. If Google/YouTube/Facebook opt in they will die, it is as simple as that. Opting in would be suicide for them, suicide.

Even if only introduced in an isolated case within a relatively small territory, say Switzerland, the UK or Belgium, Opt-In Taxation would precipitate the global downfall of a globalist corporation such as Google/Meta/Alphabet if the CEOs were foolhardy enough to jump on the cancel culture bandwagon by opting in to pay higher corporate taxes 'just in one' local geographic/economic area.

If an international social media company opts in to pay higher tax in the EU or the UK or Switzerland following Opt-In Taxation being introduced into those places, the US and Canadian and Australian investors in that social media company will instantly, within only a few short hours, sell every last share they own in the social media company in question.

What would likely occur in reality, in practice, is every corporation refusing to ever opt in, in any way, which would save the corporation from near sudden-death, keep the share price sky high, and maintain the great lifestyles and quality of life enjoyed by the CEOs and early investors who have profited much by the corporations endeavouring to keep corporate taxation as low as possible consistently year after year via a myriad of Machiavellian and crafty means (think lobbying and political donations). In so doing, they would succeed in once and for all killing wokeism and fascist cancel culture and the collective sharing of suffering and severe class/tax inequality. No longer benefiting from their relationships with wokeists and wokevists and progressive liberals and social justice warriors, the corporations would insist to governments everywhere that they and their business interests now be protected from cancel culture bullies and boycotters, with individuals and individuals alone who identify as internationalists and liberals and progressives and woke being those who choose to opt in to pay higher taxes, creating equality, enabling everyone to get exactly what they want.

Corporations can continue to make money—the sole reason they exist, "charity" and "virtue" and "ideals" and "mission statements" will all finally fall by the wayside as the true beast of capitalism is seen when looking upon the "benevolent and progressive and fun" Silicon Valley tech companies who all, each and every one, flatly refuse to pay a dime more in tax than is absolutely necessary.

The poor and the conservative and the libertarian and the nationalist will all opt out, which puts more money in their pockets, which they can invest in shares, which they can invest in land or property or use to purchase goods and services, aiding economic growth and new industries and enterprises and opportunities.

Woke liberals and individual millionaires/billionaires can impoverish themselves to help foreign causes/peoples/nations or to ensure that everyone who demands methadone can get methadone.

Upon the enactment of Opt-In Taxation, either corporations will die or class/tax inequality and globalisation will die.

Chapter Thirty-Seven—Food for Thought

'I was literally singing to myself on my way home, after the killing. The, tension, the desire to kill a woman had built up in such explosive proportions.'
—David Berkowitz, who pled guilty to perpetrating eight shootings, killing six.

This is where additional points, insights and snippets of education have ended up.

This series of eight books (the eighth being a compilation of the first seven) is, I believe, long enough already without extending each of the following short sections into chapters or books in their own right.

***

<u>Shared Values</u>

When the capital punishment debate begins, a debate that is long overdue, elites of various stripes will immediately counter with, 'Capital punishment is against our shared values.'

Facts: There is no unity at the present time, no shared values whatsoever, evidenced by their being voter apathy, hundreds of millions of people across the Western world who rarely if ever vote, with incidents such as Brexit being rare exceptions, where folk who never, and had never in many instances, voted came out in droves to vote for greater freedom, autonomy and sovereignty and responsibility and self-control and duty and pride despite the 'remain side' employing vast resources and incredible propaganda and scare tactics as a means to prevent people power and democracy from being done—"shared values" was mentioned much then. This term is meaningless; there is currently no unity whatsoever.

At the present time in Canada, the USA, Germany, the UK, France, Australia and many other Western democracies folk are disunited and segregated; they feel separate, with only elites and those at the top of the pyramids in these lands claiming we all have "shared values".

For instance, millions of recent Muslim migrants (in the EU and the UK) want death for non-criminal homosexuals. We need to dispense with the absurd lie that the British people, American people or any people within the framework of consumerist, capitalist, debt-based societies are currently one and united. We are fractured; we are dying. The dream of having a servile sheep class forever who dance to the liberal, capitalist, globalist tune is dead. To the average native working man, most native political elites who speak of "shared values" might as well be aliens as they are so foreign in every way that matters.

Do not tell us what our values are if you refuse to hold referendums on voluntary taxation and capital punishment as well as an open debate on prison and probation reform.

And when you observe big business and politicians attempting to stop the capital punishment and voluntary taxation referendums, please know the reason why—because with the introduction of these things true equality is created due to corporations and liberal elites now having to pay higher taxes in order to fund prisons, probation, refugee causes and foreign aid.

Voluntary taxation means you only pay for what you want, what you need. Immigration, refugees, socialised medicine, prisons, rehabilitation of terrorists and paedophiles—once the referendum date is set, say goodbye to ever having to pay a penny to fund these things as, after the vote, only the wealthiest and those who benefit the most from the system will have to open their purses and wallets.

***

The Hypocrisy of Criminals and Woke Activists

Ask a convicted murderer who raped and killed three young girls, who is awaiting execution as he and every liberal woke individual on the planet demands he is not executed, whether or not he would want the state to kill the man who raped and killed his mother, sister or daughter tomorrow.

The answer surely will be, 'Of course that man should die if he raped and killed a member of my family!'

Those who believe in equality must treat the rapists and murderers of this world in the same way the rapists and murderers would have you treat those who hurt or destroyed their family. Why should there be a difference? Wouldn't that be hypocritical?

Ask a home invader how he would react if three heavily armed violent thugs smashed their way into his house and began stealing all of his possessions whilst threatening to kill him if he dared to get out of his bed.

Would the home invader, who was having a night off, suddenly change his ways and demand that, 'Violent home invaders should be executed'?

Perhaps he will think this in the moment as the invaders beat him, perhaps torture him for his debit card pin code, and rape his wife in front of his eyes, but he would only want this punishment to apply to those who have hurt him, who have wronged him and his family—because every violent criminal is a hypocrite and a user. Live by the sword, die by the sword.

***

Parole Board

It should be stated to every individual who has a deciding vote on whether or not prisoners of any category are released from custody that, rather than imagining freeing people into the wilderness, rather than thinking the prisoners are being released into a metropolis or big system with many cogs and components, instead, every single time, they should imagine that prisoner coming to live with them, their children and their grandchildren all together in the same big happy and fluffy and very liberal house.

If the psychotherapist, probation officer, governor, priest and whoever else may sit on such a parole board panel would never desire the prisoner to come within 100 miles of their home or family that individual must be remanded in prison or euthanized as not to do so is to knowingly and willingly release a very dangerous (and now aggravated due to loss of liberty and hurt pride) offender upon the unprotected and unaware and unsuspecting general population—just so that those on the board don't have to say 'no' to the sad face pleading his or her case.

It's easier to give people what they want and giving folk second chances makes inferior, weak fools feel suddenly virtuous and benevolent and powerful, almost godlike in their ability to 'save a life' or grant clemency/amnesty and a second, then third, then fourth, then one hundredth chance.

This stupidity and weakness must end.

***

Unimaginable Pain, Terror and Suffering

If you think capital punishment a 'step too far' I refer you to the cases of Colonel Russell Williams in Canada and Myra Hindley and Ian Brady in the UK.

Spend just a few minutes reading the overview of these two instances of inhuman monsters destroying many lives and I'm certain you will very quickly change your mind in relation to capital punishment being necessary for those who may indeed look like you but are something altogether different inside, where it counts.

If you read what Brady did and what Williams did and afterwards would happily consent to these men coming to live in your community, be happy for them to live in the next house or apartment to you and would be happy for them to freely sit on a park bench in your local neighbourhood, it suggests you want to defend even the most brutal sadists and unrepentant monsters in our midst. However, if you want these men kept one million miles away from you, for all time, you will either have to personally pay much higher taxes to keep such folk behind lock and key or you must allow real justice to be done by welcoming capital punishment as both a deterrent and means to make safe your community for all time.

In the case of Williams, not only will liberal Canada grant him freedom one day, the liberal Canadians will also soon be paying this man a huge pension each year in recognition of his military service, and due to his rank being that of colonel, his pension will be really quite large. Williams will also require state-funded housing likely, state protection, a new identity and much else, all provided by taxpayers, the same taxpayers he previously preyed upon, terrorised and literally raped and tortured.

This is why I am illiberal and pro capital punishment. It's not because I like evil and killing; no, it's because I wish to end evil and killing. I wish to stop all the Williamses of this world offending; I wish to stop reoffending, and once the offending and reoffending is halted, no legal euthanasia of men like Brady and Shipman and Bundy and Williams will be needed.

Currently, such folk know full well that the 'worst that can happen' as a result of their crimes and inhumanity is twenty years' free accommodation in prison before being released on a full pension with a new identity and huge freedom. What a joke of a system. Victims deserve justice; victims-to-be need us all to be strong, strong as iron.

***

Vote at Home

If you claim to be opposed to euthanizing serial killers, paedophiles and terrorists; if you state that, 'If given the opportunity, I would certainly vote against capital punishment,' what you can do, until such a time as the people are entrusted to have their say on this crucially important issue, is vote at home, now, right now. Get a pen or pencil and a piece of paper and you can cast your vote immediately.

Voting at home is a symbolic gesture, yet it serves to confirm or validate your internal ethics, beliefs and morals. Here is an example of how you could vote at home if you so chose. If you believe you are 'in the right', please vote now, with me and with everyone else.

Choose a day of the year to vote (perhaps today, perhaps right now) and then vote each year at home in the same way as described below because until the people are permitted a referendum on this issue, this is as close as you can come to feeling as though you have power, a say, or are in control of your destiny and able to protect your family and community to the best of your ability.

You may choose to vote today or on January 1st, whatever day you choose; repeat the same action each year, writing down on a piece of paper the following. Either:

I choose to vote against capital punishment for killers, rapists, paedophiles, terrorists, spies, traitors, fifth columnists, violent predatory criminals and corrupt politicians and civil servants.

Or:

I choose to vote in favour of capital punishment for killers, rapists, paedophiles, terrorists, spies, traitors, fifth columnists, violent predatory criminals and corrupt politicians and civil servants.

Once your "vote is cast", keep that little piece of paper somewhere safe as the next time there is a terror attack, violent gang crime, a home invasion that escalated to a murder; the next time people in your community become victims of sexual assault; the next time crime waves and disorder and fear spread through your land, you will know that none of this is your fault if you voted in favour of capital punishment and, as a result, latterly informed one and all that you support capital punishment, justice and the rope as a deterrent and a means to get justice for victims whilst safeguarding the community.

Yet, if you are a parent and wrote down, 'I vote against capital punishment, I am a proud pacifist,' and after you voted that way at home your child or children become the victims of serious crime, perhaps they are even the victims of carjackers, home invaders, rapists or murderers or terrorists, you must agree that you cannot complain, that you have no right to be angry whatsoever, as being a pacifist around bullies will always lead to you and your family being bullied. Being weak and passive invites domination by the unrighteous; being liberal and soft on crime will condemn your entire family to a bleak, fear-filled existence of merely hoping that they will not become victims again and again and again.

It is one thing thinking that you would vote against euthanizing unrepentant and unrehabilitable murderers, serial killers, terrorists and paedophiles; however, once compelled to write down your voting choice at home, and keeping that ballot in your home, where your children sleep, supposedly protected by you, by your love, by your strength, by your duty and honour and loyalty and humanity, you may discover that a terrible taste forms in your mouth suddenly as the smile leaves your face, because if you place that homemade ballot under your baby's crib, what kind of father or mother does that make you? A nihilist? An extreme masochist? A coward? Or all three?

If you are still, after these tens of thousands of words, committed to being pacifistic and tolerant and forgiving and self-abnegating and desiring to pay higher taxes to keep the scum of the earth in prison forever, bankrupting yourself and the community in so doing, please, please do not laugh at the suggestion of voting at home. By all means, mock this book, leave terrible reviews for it, seek to ban it even because it contains opinions you disagree with, but please do not ignore the home-voting suggestion. Please write down your choice now, immediately, whether or not you have children and dependants.

Please be honest. Please write down your choice immediately and afterwards look at yourself in the mirror.

***

It Is Rarely the Case That a Person Made a Mistake

Rapists and paedophiles, home invaders and violent criminals and serial killers stalk their victims, sometimes for hours, days, even weeks, including extensive grooming and psychological manipulation and bullying (in the case of sexual offenders). They often threaten to kill victims and their families if they report the abuse.

Some people cannot be "fixed" as there is nothing to fix because they were born different to the majority. They are unable to tell the difference between fake tears and real tears, fake fear and real fear, for instance.

Sometimes people make mistakes; yet, when it comes to all violent crime and serious crimes such as premeditated murder, terrorism and sexual offences, the only mistake was the perpetrator getting caught.

I want to believe people can change, that everyone can change, even the man who abuses children; yet the reality is that cunning, Machiavellian men and women will insist they "found God", 'mended their ways', 'have seen the light' and have had 'the evil educated out of them'. In truth, as recidivism rates prove undeniably, the only way to stop paedophilia is to remove a man's testicles or to euthanize him. Until that point he is a mortal danger to every child, just as every murderer, terrorist and rapist about to be released into your tolerant liberal (soft) nation in 2024/2025 and beyond is of course an extreme danger to you, your family, your neighbours and everyone else.

Some dogs are rabid and require immediate euthanasia in order to protect the community. The same is true of humans.

***

The Difference Between Woke liberals and Unwoke Illiberals

The unwoke illiberal ignores the complaints of the man who killed the child he raped when he speaks of being "sad and lonely" in his prison cell, taken away from all he knows and all his creature comforts, but the woke liberal wants to hold his hand and soothe him, wants to provide him comfort and nurture and solace, wants to listen to his excuses for his inhumanity and hear him blame-shift to others. That is the difference.

The woke liberal immediately, absolutely immediately, forgives their son for raping an infant and offers them protection and comfort and love and help, whereas the unwoke illiberal immediately disowns, disinherits and disavows their son if he rapes an infant and afterwards informs the authorities and the community that a terrible danger exists in their midst, a danger that should be hurriedly euthanized or enjoy a fifty-year life extension thanks to the subset of citizens and business owners and members of the clergy who desire to fund the life extensions of rapists and killers and paedophiles. Woke liberals love their criminal children; unwoke illiberals no longer have a child if the child commits violent crime.

***

$1000

When a convicted rapist from a small village is euthanized (after raping 100 women or boys or girls over a period of time, destroying innumerable lives and traumatising so many people), in effect everyone in the village receives a $1000 gift as that is what they would have had to pay to keep the rapist in prison and away from vulnerable and innocent folk if the repeat offender had been sent to prison, afterwards entering the probation system and requiring welfare and free housing and all else for many years after.

That one individual would cost the taxpayers millions throughout the course of his life, meaning the $1000 gift represents the tax that each villager would have had to pay in additional tax to fund the life extension and happiness and comfort and food and utilities and housing for the rapist who destroyed 100 lives or more.

What would you prefer if your daughter was murdered or your grandmother or your neighbour was murdered, who was too trusting and altruistic and compassionate when helping those lost to fentanyl and heroin, several of whom raped and killed her?

Do you want to receive two $1000 cheques as a result of the two drug addicts disgracing and killing your daughter, friend or neighbour, whose cats you have now adopted, which are eternal reminders of the heinous crime being committed, or do you want to receive no cheques and for those two people to instead live for another fifty years in relative luxury and safety because you have instead chosen to write two $1000 cheques because you wish to help and support and soothe and protect those who raped and killed your loved ones?

***

Assisted Dying

If you accidentally run over a pheasant and it is terminally injured, if you support human euthanasia (because you hate unnecessary human suffering) you will instantly end the pheasant's suffering—but if you're anti-euthanasia you will drive away and ignore the suffering as your preference is extended suffering, rather than ending pain and suffering and misery and anguish swiftly and painlessly.

It is a mercy to end the life of a suffering animal whose injuries guarantee death shortly thereafter. If there is no hope of survival, euthanasia is a mercy, whereas to do nothing is to be the cause of the animal's extended unnecessary suffering.

Many who oppose human euthanasia do so to protect themselves psychologically, fearing being grief-stricken, depressed and mindful of their own mortality if their unhappy and sick relatives, friends and neighbours were able to receive state-assisted or state-approved euthanasia as a means to end their suffering.

The ethics and morality of those who are fervently opposed to euthanasia for folk with chronic depression and loneliness, Alzheimer's, dementia, cancer and degenerative disorders of all kinds and chronic pain are the same folk who wish to (in a "saviour" sort of way) extend the lives of terrorists and paedophiles and traitors.

On the surface, it may seem odd that a person who refuses to assist their relative in dying peacefully in, for instance, Switzerland or another land where assisted dying is legal (as it should be globally) also wishes to extend the life of killers and rapists, yet one should not at all be surprised as the end result of their actions on both occasions is the same—the multiplication of suffering.

Grandmother wishes to die for a multitude of reasons, for her life is pain, her unnaturally long life has birthed new, terrible conditions. She rarely recognises herself in the mirror, the pain in her knees and hips is extreme, and the liberal democracy she lives within releases violent muggers and rapists and terrorists every single day of the week, which terrifies her because she can barely walk, she is defenceless completely and loathes being a burden on her family and on the community, for she so loves them both.

Her children and grandchildren wish for her to remain alive, despite her desire to be euthanized. Her motivation is ending suffering, which means that going against her will, forcing her to remain alive, is the cause of the extension of her suffering and fear and terror and misery.

The multi-time rapist murderer does not want to die, nor does he want to stay in prison for a second longer than he has to; he wishes to be released so he can continue hurting and abusing people.

The children and grandchildren (of the suffering grandmother), despite standing against her will and wishes, do not stand against the will of wishes of the unrepentant rapist killer because this family (other than Granny) are woke privileged liberals, full of guilt and who want to believe that everyone can always live forever and the whole world is a soft, fluffy place where nothing bad really happens and death is just make-believe.

The children and grandchildren agree with the rapist murderer that he should hurriedly be released from prison and not euthanized, why?

Is it because they wish to decrease the criminal's suffering? No, because legal euthanasia can be swift and painless, as is the case in the clinics in Switzerland in 2024, and euthanizing the threat to their grandmother and to themselves would ensure:

Lower taxes (due to no extended prison stay and costly probation service)

Safer streets (one less rapist killer on the prowl)

No repeat offences (due to the killer's heart no longer beating)

In both cases, the family chooses to increase suffering, making Grandmother suffer for decades longer whilst inflicting great suffering on all of the public as a result of releasing Barabbas into the community.

Is it irresponsibility when you refuse to euthanize a dying animal, dereliction of duty, cowardice, sadism—or is it all of these things?

For a certainty it is not love when choosing to inflict more suffering by doing nothing, by preventing Granny from flying to Switzerland, by leaving a half-dead animal in the road rather than being brave and stoic and honourable by euthanizing (by whatever means) the suffering creature who suffers needlessly and it is of course not a loving gesture when moronically releasing paedophiles and serial killers and terrorists into the community.

Selfish cowards, irresponsible egotists and sadists are the only ones who ignore suffering and are the only ones who stand against capital punishment and against euthanasia.

Capital Punishment Conclusion

'When this monster entered my brain I will never know, but it is here to stay. How does one cure himself? I can't stop it, the monster goes on, and it hurts me as well as society. Maybe you can stop him. I can't.'

—Dennis Rader, known as the 'BTK Killer' (a nickname he suggested for himself, which stands for Bind, Torture, Kill), who killed ten people via suffocation or strangulation.

We were too premature when we abolished capital punishment, far too premature, as, at that time, little was known about psychopaths, dark triads or criminal psychology in general—nor did this new strain of international terrorism exist at that time.

When a hangman or executioner ends the life of a rapist or murderer or corrupt politician or drug dealer, there is no hate within him or her, it is not personal. They are doing their duty, much like the solider, the defender; they are enacting the will of the people, the popular will—the vast majority of families of victims would vote for capital punishment, if such a vote or referendum were offered to the people.

There is no hate in this book, yet there is hate and recklessness and irresponsibility to be found in releasing dangerous criminals into your community where your children live, who will for a certainty become victims in a multitude of ways as a result of reckless gambling and 'hoping for the best'.

It is not love to release a killer python or tiger into your community or a rabid dog with rabies; no, that would be hate, hatred for yourself and your friends, family and children. A paedophile who wishes to kill children, a serial killer cannibal is no different from a python or rabid dog, no different whatsoever. To be against capital punishment is to hate humanity; it can be no other way.

If you loved humanity, you would kill rapists and drug dealers and corrupt politicians as your act of self-defence would save many lives and prevent much misery. When you ignore murders, rapes, paedophilia, corruption and treason, you are encouraging more of the same; you are begging to be abused and used and overtaxed and burdened by psychopathic and sociopathic life-sucking leeches who will bleed you dry before destroying you mind, body and soul. Wake up, good people, awake from your slumber. Defending killers does not prove you love. Wanting paedophiles to live in your house with you and your family doesn't prove you are full of love; it absolutely proves you hate yourself and want to be destroyed.

Weakness and cowardice invite crime and violence, whereas strength and courage end crime and violence.

When the people become fatigued by disorder and surrendering to the predatory and uncivilised few, the death penalty shall return everywhere as its absence is not proof of civility, evolution and societal perfection but of dereliction of duty, hedonism, individualism, irresponsibility, weakness and apathy—and it is no coincidence that criminals posing as business people and criminals posing as politicians are vehemently opposed to capital punishment as these groups, just like the dark elements hiding within many clergies, are of course self-serving and seeking protection for their number when they staunchly oppose the rope, the guillotine or the firing squad.

Beyond all the arguments listed herein, which prove, I believe, the necessity for capital punishment in every nation, there is truly only one argument needed, and that is: <u>It is natural for any species to kill predators.</u>

In an ant colony, a rogue ant that hurts or kills his fellow ants shall be put to death by the majority; the same is true in wasp societies and the same is true with bears, lions, giraffes, dolphins, and kangaroos.

No (sane and free) species tolerates destructive internal fifth-columnistic forces hurting, raping and killing wantonly without a fierce immediate righteous and glorious backlash, which renders the offender unable to ever again commit harm and proliferate fear and disorder and unrighteousness.

Does the lioness call for tolerance and progressive liberalism and understanding and therapy and rehabilitation when witnessing an adult male lion attempting to breed with or violently attack one of her young cubs?

No, she risks her life immediately as she puts herself between her innocent cub and the violent, sadistic, psychopathic, mentally ill attacker—and the only lions that will attempt to prevent her from killing the offender attacking her babies are traitors to their species, are self-hating lions, are fools, are scoundrels and thus will be shunned by the majority, shunned by nature, shunned by God.

Forget silly arguments against capital punishment for a moment, such as 'What if he's innocent?' as CCTV, DNA, polygraphs and confessions render this a moot point, null and void in fact in the vast majority of cases, and just focus instead on the violent, murderous rapist who leads police to where the bodies are buried. We need to make the starting point here; we need to ask those who use arguments such as, 'What is he's innocent?' if they desire to kill a proven and unapologetic, non-empathic killer and rapist. The answer will be NO—which proves that all arguments used against the death penalty are merely cognitive dissonance, merely an attempt to create the wrongful and inaccurate impression that there are so many separate and insurmountable reasons as to why we shouldn't have capital punishment that those who demand real justice, accountability and good order, peace and harmony should just shut up and accept their fate of continually becoming victims.

Ultimately, once each and every micro-argument (all made in desperation) has been defeated, wild emotion and biblical references and an insistence that the unrepentant murderous rapist is 'a person to who has a right to life' will be used in a last-ditch attempt to "win"; yet when the anti-death penalty lobby win, we all lose as their brand of self-hating and self-abnegating masochism spreads far and wide, as homes get new locks and new alarm systems and children become implanted with GPS trackers in order to track them down when they are inevitably kidnapped by the predators so protected by the virtuous vocal few who insist that the only murders that can occur in the nation are those committed by the people they advocate for and protect.

Would a rapist try to rape you if they knew for a certainty that if caught they would be hung within thirty days? Once proven guilty, there should be no decades-long death row nonsense as seen in some nations; the guilty should be removed from existence as soon as practically possible, as would be the case in an ant colony, as would be the case in a pride of lions, as should be the case in any sane and well-functioning society and civilisation.

We should kill those who will continue hurting us not because it brings us pleasure and joy, as it should not; we do this not to be happy but to prevent abject trauma and misery from multiplying exponentially as rapists, paedophiles and mass murderers are permitted to replicate themselves as they are tolerated and accepted back into civilised society, which they continually bring into disrepute.

Love thy neighbour, yes, until he rapes your daughter; then you end his life. If you do not, he will rape your son also, then your nephews and nieces, before he kills some of your relatives.

We can live in a fantasy dream world of fakery where the tooth fairy, Easter bunny and Santa are real or we can grow up, become Homo sapiens and with an iron fist restore peace and good order everywhere, make safe our streets and purge our communities of the destructive non-empathic and psychopathic antisocial elements that will never change, never learn and never stop abusing the tolerant and progressive, bleeding-hearted do-gooders who continuously fight and advocate for them.

If your son is a rapist or murderer or a corrupt or treasonous politician, you must consider him dead to you and move on with your life in strength. The whole comes first; the community comes first. Do not love and protect the wicked or the criminal, even if he shares your surname, even if you have nurtured and loved the killer or rapist or hard drug pusher or corrupt representative who is destroying his nation.

Being passive and masochistic and liberal and tolerant is easy, it is lazy, and it is inglorious, low and not in keeping with the high achievements of our peoples.

But being active, responsible, illiberal and intolerant of repeat offenders and rapists and murderers destroying your green and pleasant land is glorious, righteous and true to nature, our instinct and our epic ongoing purpose—to remain at the top of the food chain, to keep rising and becoming stronger and more evolved in every way, which does not mean allowing violent criminal offenders to eat us for dinner. No, it means pushing them out of existence the moment they dare lift a hand against civilisation, peace and our beloved innocent children.

***

Are You Dangerous?

If you would kill an attacking wolf to protect your child but demand the release of paedophiles from prison who you wish to live in your home with you and your children, you are seriously, dangerously mentally ill and unfit to be a parent or guardian.

If you would kill a paedophile on a desert island if the population was you, him and your son or daughter but DEMAND every paedophile is released from prison in your nation ASAP, it means you are happy to risk the lives of other people's children as well as your own, which makes you dangerous, a hypocrite and severally cognitively dissonant.

***

Crime Dependency and a Failed System

The absence of strong and decisive leadership on the issue of capital punishment and safeguarding our children from the numerous threats abounding in society is the direct cause of mass criminality, with the system as it currently exists 100% reliant on crime and criminality to continue to exist as so many industries have sprung up around crime and disorder, for instance:

The media in its present form: They primarily report on crime, corruption, sleaze, violence, etc.

The judiciary: Many judges, barristers, lawyers, stenographers and security guards rely on crime continuing in order to keep being paid.

The police: In a crime-free nation, the police would primarily focus their attention upon policing politicians and other public servants.

The prison service: With people too afraid to commit crime, prisons would be closed, resulting in quite a few job losses, including for the businesses that provide locks, keys, bars, meals for prisoners, health facilities for prisoners and education/re-education for prisoners.

The probation service: No crime means no need for probation officers, no more electronic ankle bracelets needed and a whole host of people and service providers who will all become unemployed.

If crime ends, so will no fewer than one million jobs in the UK and perhaps five million jobs or more in the USA. What an insane situation. We must manoeuvre away from this absurd reality of 'needing crime to continue' in order to prevent a rise in unemployment. Gradually prisons must close, gradually sentences must increase and immediately the people must be able to have a say on the reintroduction of capital punishment because they were not allowed a voice or vote when it was abolished; if they were, it would still remain today in every land, guaranteed.

It is in the interest of the people for crime, especially violent crime against the individual, to end today; yet there are many parties with vested interests as detailed above who would be inconvenienced in the short-term in the event of a 100% peaceful and harmonious society being created. Judges do not want to till soil, senior police officers do not want to till soil, wardens of prisons do not want to till soil and the owners of companies manufacturing GPS ankle bracelets for released dangerous criminals do not want to till soil.

***

If you disagree with every word in this book, thanks for your time. I much appreciate you listening to a different opinion and I hope you will volunteer to pay more taxes to fund law and order, prisons and probation as well as volunteer to house unrepentant convicted murderers and rapists and drug dealers and terrorists in your home in the very near future.

If, however, you agree with everything, or at least the majority of what has been said in this book, if you put victims first each and every time, I urge you to contact your political representatives, journalists, clergy, and business owners small and large and inform them that you desire a people's vote/referendum on two issues first and foremost and your support for these referendums (you would explain to these people) comes from you being non-racist, non-classist and a lover of fair play, duty and justice—non-racist and non-classist because if capital punishment is reintroduced and if voluntary taxation is introduced, neither change hurts any race, religion, class or gender more than any other. It is true equality.

Opt-In Taxation Conclusion

'All of a sudden I realized that I had just done something that separated me from the human race and it was something that could never be undone. I realized that from that point on I could never be like normal people … It was like I crossed over into a realm I could never come back from.'
—David Gore, American serial killer who committed six murders.

It will be a brave or stupid politician who tells prospective voters, 'Sorry, but you are not permitted to have a referendum on either capital punishment or Opt-In Taxation'—this is a surefire way to guarantee your early retirement from politics.

As poverty soars, as individual debt skyrockets (Americans for instance are currently in 1.14 trillion dollars of credit card debt alone), as self-sabotaging addictions and migrant crises multiply and as demographic change and mass immigration causes friction here, there and everywhere, something has got to give as in addition to all that irks the citizen are added ever higher taxes, stealth taxes, ever more sleaze and political corruption and failed leadership.

Folk don't mind the occasional immigrant and the occasional tax hike when the sun is shining; the occasional roadblock is to be expected.

Yet, in tandem with inflation and exorbitant prices in stores and physically unpayable personal debts and loans and mortgages and car repayments and credit card and overdraft debt and student debt, huge taxes that fund the lifestyles of those who have never worked, who refuse to work and who instead prefer to rape, rob, kill and pilfer from the treasury or subsist parasitically is the final straw.

Yes, the citizen should have avoided living beyond their means; yes, the citizen should have voted more wisely in the past; yes, the citizen should have previously demanded local jobs, land and housing for local people first and foremost to ensure his and his family's solvency and happiness and sanity were maintained; yet, who can resist the slick Machiavellian advertisements offering "free money" (credit)? Who can resist the tempting mistresses that are unrestrained consumerism, groupthink and peer pressure?

The damage is done, the people are hurt, and now they find themselves living unrewarding, pointless lives whereby they try in vain to merely pay off the interest they owe to some globalist corporation or other who've no doubt been bailed out by the taxpayer at some previous juncture.

If you are on the bottom, you are not deemed 'too big to fail' by politicians; rather, you are deemed 'too small to matter' because arrogant and hubristic short-sighted politicians in this era of advertisements and political donations believe the end result of every election is predetermined as a result of how much money will be spent by party A or party B.

Removing the need for citizens to pay any tax whatsoever would not be immediately advisable as this disconnects the individual from the community, from the nation, and from the tribe; however, voluntary taxation could most certainly be incorporated into the majority of democratic nations, with many categories of taxation being based around the easy-to-understand principle of opting in to pay for additional services/departments/foreign aid, etc.

If you are a patriot yet incredibly poor and in massive depressing debt, the last thing you desire is for a very large tax demand to come through your door as, suddenly, you will not feel half as patriotic, half as loving toward the nation or people; rather, you will come to hate the government, hate politicians and blame them for every problem in your life small and large.

Allowing good, decent, hardworking and honourable folk the opportunity to pay for what they want, pay for what they use, and opt out of paying for that which they find unconscionable or bad will mean that, overnight, poverty and misery shall decrease and along with those things antisocial behaviour and so much hate for politicians and government and democracy.

Finally we will know how all feel about every topic; finally we will know the truth; finally we will be able to service every single citizen in the way they need to be and desire to be serviced by a caring and empathic and protective state.

The only argument against Opt-In Taxation, the sole argument that would drive political representatives (public servants) and career civil servants to object to the implementation of Opt-In Taxation would be:

'But won't that give the people power and control? Shouldn't we be the ones making the rules, not them?'

No one will say this aloud, of course, yet every individual who stands against this common sense reform, this just, fair and pro-people-power measure, will certainly be thinking this as they shake their heads, as they disappoint their voters and supporters whilst "apologising" for not being able to allow people to opt out of funding border walls, refugee centres or foreign aid or abortions.

Opt-In Taxation is a test case, it is the litmus test that will prove whether Brexit was a fluke, merely a one-off event of mass people power and optimism and enthusiasm for self-governance and independence and strength, or whether all democracies shall now lurch towards true representative democracy, the devolution of power and the raising up of every single citizen of every class and political persuasion as each and every man and woman is able, for the first time in history, to choose how the fruits of their labours are distributed.

I support referendums in all democracies for voluntary (Opt-in) taxation, for capital punishment, for globalisation/international continued co-dependence rather than independence and self-sufficiency, and you should too, if you truly care about people and if you wish to reduce waste, stress, anger, frustration, political corruption, recidivism and your tax bill.

If the argument against holding a referendum on Opt-In Taxation is, 'The people don't know what's good for them, they are too stupid to know how to vote, they are sheep, morons,' I say, 'Long have folk trusted politicians and civil servants and educated benevolent leaders and guardians to steer the nations and the will of all and yet all around crime and corruption and failure and obesity and drug epidemics and wars abound; are these ills caused by hardworking, humble "moron" taxpayers? Is this the bus driver's fault, the soldier's fault, the gardener's fault, the nurse's fault, the mechanic's fault? Hell no, hell no; it is the fault of those who call taxpayers 'too stupid to be able to vote on capital punishment and Opt-In Taxation.'

It is time for one and all to be responsible; it is time for a return to strength and self-discipline and duty; it is time for Opt-In Taxation; it is time for people power. If not now, when? If not now, why not? Because we are too dumb or because the gravy train will then be over? Because then the swamp shall be drained; there will be fewer cushy government jobs, the pigs will have to take their snouts out of the champagne trough and get a real job, do actual work for a living, contribute and improve rather than taking whilst limiting democracy and taking away rights and power whilst increasing taxation exponentially.

The easiest way to cause a revolution is to deny folk democracy, deny referendums. The easiest way to prevent revolutions is to give folk more democracy, more referendums—more freedom, more power, and thus more respect.

About the Author

Bruce Masters is a British author, psychologist, and optimist, a campaigner for democracy and peace, and a campaigner against globalisation and political and religious extremism.

A prolific author, Masters has written over 50 books spanning multiple genres: political, psychological, self-help and sociological as well as fiction, hoping to improve, educate and inspire.

In addition to being known for his revolutionary Peace Book series (including *Six Ways to Prevent WWIII* and *How We Will Create Peace in Ukraine and the World*) and his Capitalism and Democracy series of books Masters is a leading researcher and writer in the fields of autism, neurodivergence and atypicality. His suite of books relating to these subjects includes *Autistic Jesus, The Führer of Asperg: A New Understanding of Fascism, Autism and the Third Reich, ConjectureMania, The Christ Conspiracy, Tripartheid* and *The Continuation of the Origin of the Species.*

Bruce is a man of many talents and interests: a political observer and analyst, researcher and occasional satirist.

When not writing, he leads a quiet life with his family and is thankful for having the drive, knowledge and will required to birth so many unexpected, empathy-multiplying and thought-provoking political, psychological, and sociological works.

Bruce's books are very much like Marmite: You will either love or hate his unapologetically bombastic and forthright 'tough love' writing style and his leadership-heavy political and social critique and musings.

Yet one thing is for certain; you will not be bored as entertainment in addition to a roller coaster of education intermingled with opinion is guaranteed from beginning to end.

Books by the Author

(Published and coming soon)

The Capitalism and Democracy Book Series:
Book One The Political Lottery — Democracy's Last Best Hope of Survival
Book Two Capitalism Hates You
Book Three The Liberal Loophole Jails: A Peaceful and Righteous Revolution
Book Four The Cancellation of Coronation Street, EastEnders and the National Lottery
Book Five Why Charles Dickens No Longer Loves the White Working Class
Book Six Why The British Stopped Breeding
Book Seven How Nigel Farage Became Prime Minister
Book Eight The Soul Exchange
Book Nine Smartphones are Dumb
Book Ten The M25 Solution — The Creation of the Republic of London

The Peace Series:
Book One How We Will Create Peace in Ukraine and the World
Book Two Five Ways to Create Peace in the Middle East
Book Three Make America United Again: The Trump-Harris Co-Presidency 2024 – 2028
Book Four Plan C: Mutually Assured Survival
Book Five The Far Right and Far Left Are Far from Opposites
Book Six 10 EASY WAYS Russia Could Destroy Germany and the EU in 2025
Book Seven Six Ways to Prevent WWIII

The 33 Essential Questions Series:
Book One The Truth at Last! 33 Essential Questions for Conspiracy Theorists
Book Two The Truth at Last! 33 Essential Questions for Elon Musk
Book Three The Truth at Last! 33 Essential Questions for Prince Harry
Book Four The Truth at Last! 33 Essential Questions for Prince Andrew
Book Five The Truth at Last! 33 Essential Questions for Tommy Robinson
Book Six The Truth at Last! 33 Essential Questions for the Alt-right and Alt-left
Book Seven The Truth at Last! 33 Essential Questions for Christians

The UnWoke, Anti-Hate, Anti-Guilt Series of Books:
Book One Wokeism Is Crumbs from the Table of Globalist Elites
Book Two Wokeing Kills
Book Three Voluntary Taxation and Capital Punishment: For a Just, Equal and Corruption-Free Society
Book Four Escaping the Cult of Guilt: The Dark Side of Charity and NGOs
Book Five Defeating Fentanyl
Book Six Ending the Migrant Crisis in Europe: Preventing Class Wars, Race Wars and the Destruction of the EU
Book Seven The Sudden and Unexpected Multiculturalisation of Mayfair, Kensington and Belgravia — Which Ended Mass Immigration and White Flight in the UK
Book Eight Globalisation, Mass Immigration, Wokeism and Multiculturalism on Trial (Compilation of Books 1–7)

Psychology/Neurodivergence/Autism:
The Continuation of the Origin of the Species
Autistic Jesus
Don't Judge a Book by Its Cover: 21 Remarkable Similarities Between Donald Trump and Tommy Robinson
The List — The Death of Antisocial Behaviour and Noise Pollution and the Evolution of the Real Estate Industry
The Führer of Asperg: A New Understanding of Fascism, Autism and the Third Reich
Tripartheid
ConjectureMania
The Christ Conspiracy, aka The Rise of the Light Triads
The Truth at Last! 33 Essential Questions for Conspiracy Theorists

Biographical Exposés:
Russell Brand: False Prophet
One Election Please… How J.K. Rowling Bought British Politics, Hid Her True Self and Hoodwinked the World — an Unauthorised Biographical Exposé
The Truth at Last! 33 Essential Questions for Elon Musk
The Truth at Last! 33 Essential Questions for Prince Andrew
The Truth at Last! 33 Essential Questions for Prince Harry
The Truth at Last! 33 Essential Questions for Tommy Robinson

The Rowling Trilogy:
Book One J.K. Rowling In: It's a Kind of Magic

Book Two How Not to Get Sued by J.K. Rowling
Book Three One Election Please… How J.K. Rowling Bought British Politics, Hid Her True Self and Hoodwinked the World — an Unauthorised Biographical Exposé

Bruce Masters' One-Day Book Series:
Plan C: Mutually Assured Survival
The Liberal Loophole Jails: A Peaceful and Righteous Revolution
The American Altruist Assassin
Why The British Stopped Breeding
The List: The Death of Antisocial Behaviour and Noise Pollution — and the Evolution of the Real Estate Industry
Capitalism Hates You
Why Charles Dickens No Longer Loves the White Working Class
The Rule of Ten — How Prince Andrew Came to Be Exiled to Switzerland
The Political Lottery — Democracy's Last Best Hope of Survival

Fiction:
Plan C: Mutually Assured Survival
The Liberal Loophole Jails: A Peaceful and Righteous Revolution
The American Altruist Assassin
The Day Bill Gates Ended Crime
Wokeing Kills
The Sudden and Unexpected Multiculturalisation of Mayfair, Kensington and Belgravia — Which Ended Mass Immigration and White Flight in the UK
J.K. Rowling In: It's a Kind of Magic
The Cancellation of Coronation Street, EastEnders and the National Lottery
The Lord of Purgatory
Adrian Mackintosh: Agent of Karma
The Man in the Panama Hat
The Rule of Ten — How Prince Andrew Came to Be Exiled to Switzerland
The Soul Exchange
David Lammy on the Run — A Political Comedy Adventure
The Fall and Rise of a Comedy Legend!
Running Clear — How David Defeated Depression
David Lammy Still on the Run
Tripartheid
Unseeable
Zelenskyy
Vladimir Putin: Predestination
The Lord of Purgatory

The Political Lottery — Democracy's Last Best Hope of Survival

Non-Fiction:
How We Will Create Peace in Ukraine and the World
69 Excuses to Drink Alcohol and 1 Reason Not To
The Continuation of the Origin of the Species
Six Ways to Prevent WWIII
Smartphones Are Dumb
Why The British Stopped Breeding
Autistic Jesus
Don't Judge a Book by Its Cover: 21 Remarkable Similarities Between Donald Trump and Tommy Robinson
The List: The Death of Antisocial Behaviour and Noise Pollution — and the Evolution of the Real Estate Industry
Capitalism Hates You
The Internet vs. the Nationalnet
The Far Right and Far Left Are Far from Opposites
10 EASY WAYS Russia Could Destroy Germany and the EU in 2025
The Folly of Colonising the Stars: The Final Nail in the Coffin of AI and Space Colonisation
The Origin of African American Gangsters, Gangs and Ghettos
Five Ways to Create Peace in the Middle East
Make America United Again: The Trump-Harris Co-Presidency 2024 – 2028
How Nigel Farage Became Prime Minister
The Truth at Last! 33 Essential Questions for Conspiracy Theorists
The Truth at Last! 33 Essential Questions for Elon Musk
The Truth at Last! 33 Essential Questions for Prince Harry
The Truth at Last! 33 Essential Questions for Prince Andrew
The Truth at Last! 33 Essential Questions for Tommy Robinson
The Truth at Last! 33 Essential Questions for the Alt-right and Alt-left
The Truth at Last! 33 Essential Questions for Christians
Wokeism Is Crumbs from the Table of Globalist Elites
Why Charles Dickens No Longer Loves the White Working Class
Voluntary Taxation and Capital Punishment: For a Just, Equal and Corruption-Free Society
Escaping the Cult of Guilt: The Dark Side of Charity and NGOs
Defeating Fentanyl
Ending the Migrant Crisis in Europe: Preventing Class Wars, Race Wars and the Destruction of the EU
Globalisation, Mass Immigration, Wokeism and Multiculturalism on Trial
How Not to Get Sued by J.K. Rowling
One Election Please… How J.K. Rowling Bought British Politics, Hid Her

True Self and Hoodwinked the World—an Unauthorised Biographical Exposé
ConjectureMania
The Führer of Asperg: A New Understanding of Fascism, Autism and the Third Reich
Russell Brand: False Prophet
Noise Pollution Kills
The Christ Conspiracy, aka The Rise of the Light Triads
What Is Patriotism?
The M25 Solution — The Creation of the Republic of London
How to Quit Gambling This Week
You Have the Power